Start At The Top
Paying Dues is for Other People
Stories To Help you Succeed
By Mark Simon

Mark Simon started at the top – over and over again. As a freelancer in the entertainment industry, working on over 5,000 projects ranging from *The Walking Dead* to *Woody Woodpecker* to Nickelodeon shows, he has discovered how to jump directly into the role he wants.

Mark has landed deals with the largest realty company in the world, a job with Steven Spielberg, producing animation for Disney, closed a book deal without trying and more. He has also completely fucked up and lost amazing deals. It's all on the page for good and for bad.

This book features a series of true stories written for Mark's college-aged sons, to help inspire them…and hopefully you to advance your career.

Praise for the author's, Mark Simon, other books:

"I'll bet that if I had this book in high school, I would have finished animating a film or two. I suggest that you read this book, get to work, and do what Mark says – go make films."

- Linda S. - previously Senior VP Original Animation, Cartoon Network. Currently Senior Director of Programming, PBS Kids.

"You really can't afford to miss Mark Simon's brilliant new title Producing Independent 2D Character Animation. Simon's tome should be a constant on any aspiring animator's workstation."

- Ramin Z. - Editor, Animation Magazine.

"I just wanted to thank you for not only the terrific books you have produced, but for the amazing motivation they have instilled in me. I have many books on storyboarding, but none have provided the necessary context as your book has."

-Ben Bullock

"I have reading your book "Storyboards: Motion in Art". This is an amazing book. Congratulations. I am an artist like you. I believe you can understand me because all artists need the success, the clap of public."

-Angel Mediavilla

"I wanted to take a moment and thank you for creating such wonderful books, most specifically your Facial Expression reference series.

I am a professional Costume Designer and often teach Stage Make-Up courses at the University level-- a class in which I have often used your books as one of the primary course texts.

Thank you once again for your endless contributions and ravenous art-making. My last Stage Make-Up class has heartily sent you 34 "thumbs up."

-Mallory Prucha Rishoi

"I cannot thank you enough for writing "Producing Independent 2D Character Animation"...it has pulled me out of my depression."

- Rick S.

"Your book is here, it's a wonderful, wonderful, book. Thanks."

-Ignacio Sardiñas (Panky)

"Thanks for the great stuff! Inspirational resources!"
– Mel M.

"Mark Simon's rock-solid resume building technique was a complete eye-opening experience for me. The common sense of it all will definitely have you wondering why you didn't think of it before. Whether you're the kid fresh out of school or the veteran business executive, this book is undeniably a must-have for today's working man!"

- Christopher B.

"I purchased the book and there was a wealth of material to work with. Thank you for the time and effort into making the book. Thank you."

-Victor Claudio

"This is the most concise and comprehensive book I've seen on the subject of producing a 2D animated cartoon."

- Robert M. - Ithica, NY.

"This is by far the best book on storyboarding (Storyboards: Motion in Art) available."

- Max M.

"Your book is so informative! I can barely put it down. Anyway, I just wanted to tell you how much your book has helped so far in making my life a complete turn-around from what it was."

- Amilee H.

"Mark's presentation is the kind that makes you snap your fingers and say 'That's so obvious, why didn't I think of that?'"

-Mary Beason

Start at the Top
Paying Dues is for Other People

By Mark Simon

Mark Simon is available to speak at your event. Please see our site http://www.marksimonbooks.com/lectures/ for more details and booking.

MarkSimonBooks@yahoo.com
www.MarkSimonBooks.com

Disclaimer: *This book is written with the sole intent of expressing ideas on how to jump start your career. The stories provided are not 'the way' to advance, but are examples of what worked for the author. Luck, talent, work history and more will affect your ability to succeed. The author makes no representations, warranties or guarantees about your potential success. Come on, every situation is different, so just get inspired by these stories and then create your own.*

Forward

I started my first business when I was 12. I worked with Steven Spielberg on the biggest show on TV. I produced animation for Disney. I landed a publisher without looking for a publisher.

I did it all without working my way up through the ranks. I did it all without ever working a day in retail or ever asking "Do you want fries with that?"

But I did have a goal and a desire for each and every job or deal I went after. Passion sells.

I've been very lucky in my life. I've got a great family. I've got my health. I do what I love for a living and I make good money at it.

I work in Hollywood. I've been lucky enough to work with the best in the industry and I've worked on over 5,000 productions of everything from feature films, to TV series and commercials.

Well, maybe it's not so much luck. I work like hell to be prepared for when opportunities show themselves.

You know the old saying, "Luck is when preparation meets opportunity". I'm always ready to meet more opportunity.

What the saying leaves out is attitude. Attitude can make a huge difference in success in anything you do, whether it's managing people, looking for a job or asking for a date. Confidence is contagious. If you have a passion for something and complete confidence in yourself, others will also have confidence in you.

There's a fine line between complete confidence and being egotistical and I'm sure I've crossed that line many times. But I don't really care. When I know something, or how to do something, I know it, share it, do it and I don't couch my knowledge in pleasantries. Life's too short and I have too much to do.

My confidence has been a huge factor in my success in various areas of my life. The greatest gift my parents gave me was the feeling that I could do anything. I have no fear of failure. Luckily, they also trained me to try and excel at everything I approach and trained me well enough to do better than most.

Starting at the top, which I'll explain in a minute, leads to quick success, at least the way success is often described.

But that same confidence, as it can often be misplaced, can also be a hindrance to learning new things. More than once I've caught myself NOT learning something I needed to know because I had assumed I knew enough already. Those moments hurt.

There's also a problem with being really good at a lot of things. It can make you think you would do it better than someone else and thus may tend not to delegate and take on too much yourself. I am VERY guilty of that. It's a problem. It's best to surround yourself with people better than you and let them do their job…but you must keep control.

In various businesses and projects I've worked in, I almost always start at the top. I seem to run businesses, events and crew within hours, regardless of what I was hired to do. In this book, I will describe a number of these instances. I will try to explain why I believe I was given each opportunity and, where relevant, how this could have hurt my chances at long-term success to a greater degree.

So, what do I mean by 'Start at the Top'?

There's a number of sayings on how to succeed in business;

"Pay your dues."

"Work your way up."

"There are no shortcuts to any place worth going."
— Beverly Sills

For the most part, all of these quotes can be true, I just don't live by them.

Start at the Top means not having to work your way up from a lower position to the top position. It means not always paying your dues. It means there can be a shortcut to the job you desire.

Start at the Top means being prepared and jumping on new opportunities.

And, Start at the Top can also mean that you only approach the top person at a company for a job. Why interview with four people who can say 'No', when you really want to speak with the only person who can say 'Yes'?

Start at the Top means you take control at all times.

You want me to start in the mail room and work my way up? No way. Looking back at my life, even if I tried it, I'd be advanced to management within hours. This isn't a comment of a delusional and self-important man, it's a story I will tell through this book of how I've always jumped right into running things. I'll also share with you the time I took control of a work environment, only to be reminded quickly that it wasn't mine to take. Oh well.

Has starting at the top always benefited me? Nope. There have been a number of times where it kicked my ass, either quickly or after I realized that it had limited my potential growth.

Does that mean I'm going to go back and start at the bottom from now on?

Hell NO!

I've had a great life and it continues to get even better.

Sure, there are times when I created my own way of doing things that has varied from industry standards. At times this slowed me down, but then again, sometimes my ways are better and I've helped change the status quo. I don't care how things have always been done if it's not the best way.

When a new way is a better way, I do it the new way.

Should you start at the top? That depends on you. It works for me.

Hopefully you will be inspired by this book to either reach for the top, or at least understand the ramifications of it.

Either way, I hope you enjoy the trip. Or don't. Your choice.

Mark Simon

Preface

Start at the top, (phrase) [yoo-ar-da-**bos**]

1. Begin at a top position without working your way up through the ranks.

2. Speaking only with the owner of a potential employment company.

3. Attitude is great if you can back it up.

pro· mo· tion

[pr*uh*-**moh**-sh*uh* n] Show IPA
noun

1. advancement in rank or position.
2. furtherance or encouragement.
3. the act of promoting.
4. the state of being promoted.
5. something devised to publicize or advertise a product, cause, institution, etc., as a brochure, f reesample, poster, television or radio commercialo r personal appearance.

Table of Contents

Section 1
I Did It My Way

Do you ever look at something and say, "I could do better than that,"?

But have you ever tried 'to do better than that'?

Have you ever thought, "That's not the right way to do something"?

But have you ever tried to fix it?

Have you ever been told to do something a certain way when you knew that way was wrong?

Did you stand firm and do it your way instead?

I have. When I think I can do better, I try it. Like when I worked for an advertising agency and realized I could do a better job providing for my clients than the agency was doing.

When I've seen something I didn't think was the best process, I've created a better process. Like when I saw my father's training and selling materials at Keller Williams Realty and I created a better selling process for him.

When I was told by one of my art teachers that I needed to create a portfolio her way and I disagreed, I did it my way. She even threatened my grade to make me listen. I didn't listen.

These stories and more are on the following pages of how I did things my way when I was certain my way was the best way.

Chapter 1
Landing My Dream Job With Steven Spielberg In Just 15 Minutes

One way to start at the top is to show up in person. Emails seldom make an impression. It may not always be possible to get the right person on the phone. I landed my dream job on a Steven Spielberg TV series in 15 minutes by meeting the right people in person.

I was working for Nickelodeon at Universal Studios Orlando in 1993 when I heard that Spielberg's NBC series *seaQuest DSV* had just moved onto the Universal lot for the second season. I was a fan of a first season, which was shot in Los Angeles.

I was the second designer at Nickelodeon when we opened up the network stages on the backlot at Universal. I had been working at Nickelodeon for a number of years and was ready for a new challenge.

seaQuest coming to Orlando opened up a grand opportunity for me.

Of course I wanted to work on the series. Steven Spielberg; science fiction; biggest show on TV. What's not to love, right?

The production of *seaQuest DSV* set up in what's called Building 22A on the Universal backlot in Orlando. 22A is the central office building with rental offices for productions. My office was on the far side of the lot in the Nickelodeon building. Nickelodeon had two sound stages which were attached to the Nickelodeon offices. I was lucky I was on the same lot as Spielberg's show.

Email didn't exist then. And I didn't want to simply call and be told to mail in my resume. I had tried that before. Didn't work. I wanted on that show and I knew I had to meet the right people in person.

I figured everyone in Orlando wanted to work on the show and I needed to beat them to the punch. I had to work fast.

Like many artists and designers, I always carried my portfolio with me. (This was long before the internet, tablets or smart phones. We had to carry large printed portfolios which looked like a someone ran over a briefcase with a steamroller.)

In order to meet someone, I needed a way in. I thought about who I knew in Building 22A. Hopefully someone who might have met anyone on Spielberg's show.

Patty! She had a small office in 22A. Patty is that friend we all seem to have. The one who talks way too much to everybody. Nice enough, but a bit of a busybody.

I knew Patty probably met someone on the crew because, well, she's Patty.

So I called her up and said: "Patty. It's Mark."

"Hey Mark. How are you doing?" she replied.

"Great!" I had no time for small talk. I was on a mission. "Hey look, who do you know on the seaQuest crew?"

She replied, "Not really…But, you know two days ago I had lunch with the construction coordinator, Mike something."

"Great!" I exclaimed. "I started in the industry as a construction coordinator! I speak his language. Look, I want you to introduce me. I'll be in your office in 5 minutes."

Then I hung up quickly because I didn't want to give her a chance to say "No."

I ran across the lot and up to her office, portfolio in hand.

I was at Patty's office within about 45 seconds. She looked up at me and said, "How you doin' Mark?"

"Great, great, great, great! Let's see if we can find Mike." I said cutting her off with a smile. I was anxious.

"Um, ok," she replied hesitantly. We walked out of Building 22A between a couple of the sound stages and sure enough, there was Mike walking out of a sound stage. "Hi, Mike," she called out.

"Hi Patty. How are you doing? Blah.. blah.. " I didn't really listen to what he said to her.

Patty replied, "Hey Mike. I want you to meet a friend of mine, Mark," at which point I forgot Patty existed.

I launched into an excited conversation with my new best friend on *seaQuest*. "Mike. Hey, I heard you're the construction coordinator. I started as a construction coordinator back in LA at Roger Corman's studio."

I wanted to build a bridge with Mike as quickly as possible. "I'd love to see the sets up close. It looks like there's great stuff you're doing."

He said "Sure." We walked around one of the stages as I exclaimed how cool the sets were. I looked at Mike and said, "I'd love to get on this crew."

Mike asked me, "So what do you do?"

I told him I was currently art directing at Nickelodeon, but I figured the production would have brought the art director out from Los Angeles. I added, "But I also do storyboarding and set design. I would do anything to work on this project."

Figure 1 - Standing on a set of Spielberg's NBC series, seaQuest DSV.

I plopped my portfolio onto a pile of lumber and quickly showed him a few samples to prove I knew what I was talking about.

Mike nodded and said, "I think we need both, but I don't make those decisions."

"Great! Who does? Who should I talk to?" I asked.

"Probably Vaughn Edwards, our production designer."

The easiest way to meet people is to be introduced. I asked, "Great. Is he around?"

Mike didn't hesitate. "Um, I think so. He might be on his office."

I didn't hesitate either. "Cool. Can you introduce me?"

Now Mike paused for a moment. "Um. Sure," guy he'd never seen before.

Mike led me out of the stage and upstairs in Building 22A to Vaughn's office. Luckily Vaughn was sitting at his drafting table.

Mike walked me in and said, "Hey Vaughn. I want you to meet this great local designer and artist Mark Simon." Mike had only glanced at my work and he had just met me. But attitude is everything and my attitude obviously made an impression. As soon as Mike introduced me to Vaughn, all my attention stayed on Vaughn.

Vaughn smiled at me and said, "So what do you do?"

"I'm a set designer and I do storyboarding.

"Well, we have need for both. I'd love to see your stuff!"

Once again I laid out my portfolio. Vaughn looked everything and said, "This all looks great! But I'm not the one who makes final decision!"

Do you want to guess what I said next? "Who does?"

"That would be Oscar Costo, our supervising producer."

"Cool! Is he around?" (Sound familiar?)

"He's usually in his office."

"Can you introduce me?"

Luckily he answered, "Sure."

Vaughn walked me down to Oscar's corner office.

Oscar was in his large office. I mean a really massive office! Vaughn knocked on the open door and said, "Oscar? This is Mark Simon. He's a great local set designer and story artist. I looked at all his stuff and either one would work great for me."

Oscar looked at us for a moment and said, "OK. Thanks, Vaughn. Come on in, Mark." He waved me in as Vaughn left.

I walked in and I handed my open portfolio to Oscar. He literally just flipped through my work in a few seconds and then closed it.

Oscar looked up at me and stated very directly, "I've met a lot of people here Orlando who can design sets just like you."

That was not the way I had hoped this conversation would start.

Oscar continued, "But you are the only one around here who understands storyboarding. You're our new storyboard artist."

And just like that I was working on a Steven Spielberg series.

Within 15 minutes of deciding I wanted to work on *seaQuest DSV*, I had the job. I was then the storyboard artist on the best project I had ever worked on!

I landed the gig quickly because I approached them in person and found a way to get inside. I didn't limit myself to the standard approach of phone calls or letters. I met them in person and I demonstrated my passion. They quickly got an idea of who I was.

Any time you want to land a job, show up in person. It shows tenacity and people get to know you faster in person than any other way.

*Figure 2 - Sitting in my seaQuest office with the alien creature
I illustrated for Mark Hamill to play.*

Chapter 2
How I Landed My Job
On The Walking Dead

You have to be willing to ask for help to move ahead.

Once my kids graduated from high school, I decided to move to Atlanta to take advantage of all the great productions in Georgia. I always set goals for myself and one of my goals was to storyboard on one of my favorite shows, *The Walking Dead*.

Luckily I have worked in the industry a very long time, over 30 years. As of this writing I have over 4,500 production credits. But I still ask for help from people I've worked with.

I knew one person on *The Walking Dead*, director of photography Stephen Campbell. He and I had worked on dozens of projects together over the last 20+ years. I called Steve prior to moving to Atlanta and asked him to introduce me to the producer who hires the crew of *The Walking Dead*. I just needed an intro.

Steve suggested we wait until the series started pre-production early in the Spring of 2018. Once the production offices opened up that Spring, I planned a trip to Atlanta to both look for a home and to hopefully meet with the producers.

Once the offices opened up for the new season, Steve spoke with series executive producer Tom Luse about me and forwarded Tom's contact info to me. I immediately reached out to Tom to set up a face-to-face meeting. I spoke with Tom briefly on the phone, explained my background and the benefits of working with me. I shared with him the days I planned to be in town and we set up a time to meet.

Without Steve's help, I wouldn't have even known that Tom was the producer I needed to speak with. Without that personal endorsement, I may not have landed that meeting even if I had called Tom.

*Figure 3 - The first thing I saw when I entered
The Walking Dead studios, were the famous doors
from the first episode.*

When I arrived in town, I drove directly to the studio in Senoia, south of Atlanta, and arrived 15 minutes early. You never want being late to be their first impression.

When I sat with Tom, I pulled out my computer and explained my process of digital storyboarding and showed him examples of my work and how my Storyboard Pro software allowed me to offer more to productions.

Tom explained that they were not quite ready to hire a story artist, but he liked what he saw. He asked me to check back with him in two weeks. The way he asked me to call back in two weeks sounded like a test. I've done the same thing at my studio with applicants to see if they can follow through.

Exactly two weeks later I called Tom. He thanked me for following up and told me that one of the other producers would be in touch for me to start on the show. Later that day I got a call from another producer and was officially hired. I had passed the test.

I started storyboarding *The Walking Dead* before I finished my move to Atlanta.

There are a few morals to this story. One, be willing to ask for help. Two, meeting people face-to-face is always best. Three, try to meet with the person who can say 'Yes' so you don't give other people the opportunity to say 'No'. And four, when you are asked to do something, follow through.

You may know lots of people who are willing to help you. But unless you ask for help, they won't know you need any.

Chapter 3
How I Lost and Regained
My Book Deal

You know the old saying, "Lightning never strikes twice?" I don't agree.

I've been known to strike more than one time for any number of things. An old saying I do agree with is, "Don't take no for answer." I've done that, too.

I'm going to share with you how I lost a deal for one of my books, and then regained it.

Back in 1993 I had been working with Steven Spielberg on his NBC series *seaQuest DSV*. I was also teaching storyboarding at a couple of universities and I had started lecturing about storyboarding at various events.

I self-published a paperback, spiral bound book on storyboarding, *Storyboards: Motion In Art*. The text went along with the slides I put together for my presentation and the second half of the book was simply a reproduction of my slides. It was very simple and not very professional. It was a back-table sales product, something that I could sell after I spoke. Looking at it now, it's a piece of shit book, but it's amazing what people will buy from the speaker they just saw.

During the *seaQuest* production, I reached out to *Starlog Magazine* to see if they would be interested in running a feature about my storyboarding work. The magazine was selling a million copies per issue, so I was thrilled when they decided to run a six page article about my storyboarding. I mentioned to the editor about the storyboard book I had created and we made a deal to promote my book in the back of their magazine. They sold it, collected the money, mailed out the books and sent me a commission. I sold thousands of copies that way.

After I had worked on *seaQuest,* I wanted to write a better version of my storyboarding book, so I wrote an entirely new book.

The new version did not feature any references to my slides. The new one covered storyboarding unlike any other book on the subject. It was a thorough and proper text book on the subject.

I called the new book *Storyboards: Motion In Art, Second Edition*. Even though it was an entirely new book, I liked the original title and I thought *Second Edition* sounded good.

I researched various potential publishers and the biggest publisher of entertainment industry books at the time was Focal Press. I found a Focal Press editor who was doing books in the same realm as storyboarding, so I contacted her. She liked what I had to say on the phone and sent me their the book proposal forms to fill out. I put together a huge proposal for them and included info on my *Starlog* book sales to prove interest in the market.

I mailed her in my new book and the proposal. About two weeks later I received a written response saying, "Thank you for your book proposal. It looks good. We see that you have an earlier version of your book. Could you please send that to us so we may review that as part of your proposal."

Figure 4 - The first edition of my book, which tanked my first pitch to my publisher.

That made sense to me, so I mailed the first edition of my book to them.

After about two weeks, I got a letter from Focal Press which stated, "Thank you very much, Mr. Simon, for your submission. However, after reviewing the first edition of your book we've determined that the quality is not high enough for Focal Press production. Thank you very much and good luck with your book elsewhere."

I knew the first book wasn't very good. That's why I rewrote it.

I called the publisher to argue for my new book, but they kept telling me the same thing, "Sorry this isn't high enough quality for us."

I thought about it and realized that people can't see beyond what they have in their hands. All they saw was the crappy first edition. No matter how much better the second one was written, it wasn't yet designed, so all they could see was the crappy first edition.

I was crushed. My new storyboard book was really good. I wanted to get it published, but that first edition killed my chances.

After I'd calmed down for a few days, I thought, wait a minute, they're the biggest publisher in the field. I bet they get a lot of proposals. They probably won't remember one failed proposal from the next.

I waited about two months and then I sent them the exact same proposal for my book. I didn't even change the name. It was still *Storyboards: Motion In Art, Second Edition*.

Once again, I received a letter from them, "Dear Mr. Simon, thank you for your book proposal. It looks good. We see that you have an earlier version of your book. Could you please send that to us so we may review that as part of your proposal."

Unlike my previous response, this time I called them up and I said, "No. I'm not going to send the first edition to you. The first edition is not representative of the second edition. I don't want it to skew your view. I want you to judge the second edition on its own merits."

They argued with me for a few minutes, but I wouldn't budge. They finally replied, "Fine. We will.

Two weeks later I received a publishing contract in the mail.

I learned from my first mistake. Just because someone asks for something, doesn't mean you have to supply it.

I also learned that you can go back and pitch something as long as you have something new to show. I didn't change my book, but I did change the presentation. I removed the problem.

Any time you run into an obstacle, find a way around it. It's amazing what can happen when you don't take 'No' for an answer.

Figure 5 - My storyboard book is now in its 3rd edition and in multiple languages.

Chapter 4
I'll Take The Lower Grade, Thanks

There are times in your life when you need to go against counsel that you're given, even if you're still in school.

When I was in high school, I was lucky enough to have Roberta Sajda as my art teacher. Roberta had an unbelievable ability to train the best high school artists in the country.

The Gold Key is the highest regional honor in high school art. There are four quadrants in the United States. There are ten winners in each quadrant.

The year before I graduated high school Roberta taught two Gold Key winners. Let that sink in. In one quarter of the United States, one teacher was responsible for 25% of the winners. It was absolutely amazing. We all loved her.

Halfway through my senior year was the time for my class to put our portfolios together to enter the Gold Key Competition. Roberta told us we need to have a broad variety in our portfolio to show variety.

I disagreed. "I don't want to do that. I'm not that good at a lot of styles and my color work is weaker. I'm really good at black and white, at pencil, at charcoal, at cartooning. That's where I excel. That's what I want to put in my portfolio."

She said, "If you want to do well, you really need to show a larger variety."

I replied, "No, I don't want to do that."

We got into quite an argument about it, to the point where she was really frustrated with me. "I will drop you a letter grade if you don't put in your portfolio what I'm telling you to include."

I looked at her and said, "You do whatever you need to with my grade. I'm doing what I think is best to win this portfolio competition. I'm going to include only my best work."

I had never in my life gotten a B in art but her threat was not enough to sway me. It was one of those moments I knew better.

It made no sense to me to put in things that were half-assed or okay along with things that were great when everything in my portfolio could be great.

We were both good to our word. She gave me my first B in art, and I put together the portfolio the way I wanted it.

My final portfolio consisted of only my best work. There was very little variety in it.

And as she had done the year before she had a winner in the national Gold Key competition. It was a friend of mine, Hai On. Hai was an amazing artist. But she also, once again, had a second winner. Me.

Figure 6 - Me and Hai On at the
Gold Key awards ceremony.

I did win the Gold Key for my portfolio in my senior year. And I did it with only my best work. My art ended up on display at the Museum of Modern Art in Houston.

Figure 7 - Standing with one of my winning black and white pieces of art at the Museum of Modern Art in Houston.

There are times you need to stick to your guns, even under threat.

Luckily I understood that grades are not always important. Success and learning mean more than a grade.

I carried that thinking into college, where I didn't care about my grades as much as I cared about learning. The only reason I went to school, was to learn. Not to get a grade.

The funny thing is, concentrating on learning did help me get better grades, just like entering the portfolio contest with only my best work helped me win.

I learned two things from my portfolio battle. One, it's worthwhile to stand up and fight when you feel certain about something. No matter the threats. If you're right, you have to stand up for it.

Two, as an artist, I also realized that the only things in my portfolio should be the best that I can do.

So, for everyone else that means, if you're a musician and you're trying out for something, only play what you're absolutely best at. If you're a dancer, dance in your best routine in your favorite style. If you're an artist, put in only your best work. If you're showing a written report to somebody, showcase the one that's the best.

Always show your best. No matter what it is that you do, you'll be judged by the worst thing that you show. Because the worst thing that you show is the best people will expect. If you're willing to show it, you think it's good enough. Is every sample good enough? If you have any doubts about anything that you show, display or present, get rid of it.

One other quick thought. We're all taught to cherish the 'A' in school. You're told, "It will go on your permanent record." What a bunch of shit. No one has ever looked at my grades. In my career, no one has even asked if I have an education.

School is for learning. Your knowledge and experience are what matter. The 'B' I was given meant nothing in my life. But what I learned from that interaction, though, was invaluable.

Chapter 5
Is It Science Or Is It Art?

I'm a believer that while in school, always turn your assignments into something you love.

Here's an example. Back in high school the dreaded science fair came up. I actually enjoyed science, but this one year I really didn't want to develop a science project. I was really getting into my art and spending a month on a science project would have pulled me away from my art.

I always wanted to be an artist and had started to consider animation as a career at the same time the science fair came about. I bought a lot of books and studied animation and my dad had introduced me to someone who ran a small animation studio in Houston. I was really excited about it.

So instead of spending time just on a science project, I decided to make the best of both worlds. I thought, "Animation is a science." I came up with the idea of studying motion using animation.

In order to have something to enter in the science fair, I created a short animation. To create my presentation, I took my animation drawings, timings and production elements and presented it in such a way that looked like it was a science experiment.

Creating the animation made the fair a lot more fun to participate in. I put a lot of time and a lot of effort into it, much more than I would have if I had just built a standard science project.

I used my dad's film camera. We built our own animation stand at our house and I put together a presentation that looked amazing.

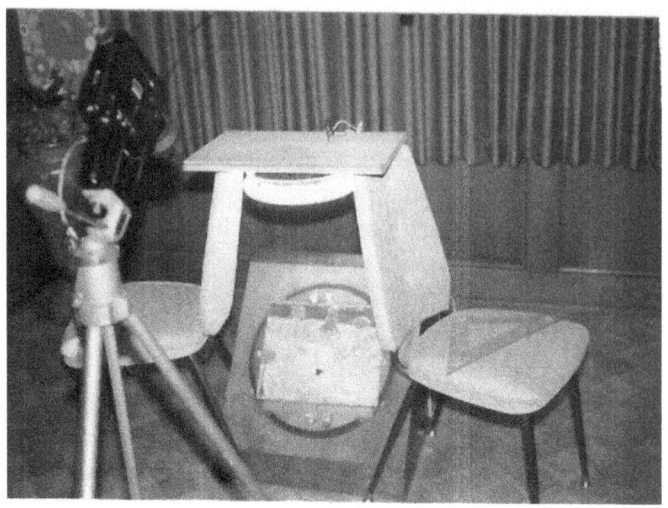

Figure 8 - The animation stand and disc Dad and I built and our setup for shooting my animation.

So there I was in a science fair with something that was realistically an art project with some science jargon…and I won. What I didn't realize was that by winning the school science fair, I had to go to the district competition.

I was one of the finalists in district and then I moved on to the State Science Fair.

At that point I was getting out of school for days at a time. It was great to play with animation and have an excuse for not going to school.

The State Science Fair in Texas was held in the Astrodome, the giant dome in downtown Houston where they hosted all the football games. It was immense. We were on the huge floor of the football field. It was a three-day event and again I make it to the finals, the top four in my division.

By the last day of the event, I knew that I couldn't get any more days off school, regardless of the results.

There was one last interview for the four of us in the finals. The other three finalists had really done an amazing job creating real science and I was there because I just wanted to draw.

One of the judges came up to me with a grin on his face and said, "Okay, what does this really have to do with science?"

I looked at him and I smiled and said, "Nothing. I just wanted to create some animation."

He looked at me, smiled big and said, "I thought so. Nice job." And he walked away.

I end up taking fourth place. I didn't place in the top three, which was fine, but I got a lot out of the entire process. One, I learned that anytime you are passionate about what you're doing you can achieve success far beyond what you expect. Two, I enjoyed it. Three, I got a great grade. Four, and probably one of the most of the important, was that I now had a sample animation for my portfolio.

I took what I had learned all the way through my high school and college years. Every assignment I was given I turned it into something I was passionate about, something supporting my career as an artist. Everything I did in school advanced my future career.

Chapter 6
Is it an English Paper
or a Job Interview?

I went to a relatively small university, Stephen F. Austin State University, SFA, in Nacogdoches, Texas. Unlike a lot of people in college, I didn't care about my grades. I had learned early on that a good and lasting education is about learning, it's not about grades.

I approached everything in college on how I could get the most out of my time and the expense of attending. In my junior year, one of my English assignments was to interview somebody in my intended career. Everyone else in the class simply found someone locally to interview. They didn't really care actually learning anything from the assignment. What a waste.

I was interested in animation. In Nacogdoches, a town of only 24,000 including students, didn't have any animation studios.

I took the assignment seriously. I figured if I was going to take the time to write a paper, why not interview somebody who could actually help me in my future career.

1984 was long before personal computers or the internet so I went to the school library and looked through the Yellow Pages for animation studios in the larger Texas cities. I had never been to Dallas so I thought finding an animation studio in Dallas was an opportunity for a road trip.

In the Yellow Pages I found an animation studio, called them up and asked to speak to the owner. He got on the phone with me and I explained to him why I called. I told him that I would like to drive to Dallas to interview him.

He replied, "Sure, as long as you come by at a time when I'm not in production."

I asked him, "Well, how about this Friday?"

That worked for his schedule, so I planned to skip a day of classes and meeting him after lunch.

The drive was about three-and-a-half hour drive from Nacogdoches to Dallas. I made my way over to his studio and showed up mid-afternoon. I was couldn't wait. I may have been the only student writing that paper who was actually excited to research his subject.

He showed me into his office and I interviewed him about directing and producing animation. It was an exciting conversation and I asked him many more questions than I had prepared. We spent more time talking than he had planned, but he seemed to enjoy my enthusiasm.

As we wrapped the interview, he offered to show me around his studio. I was thrilled to walk around and see where they created his animation. Room after room was filled with incredible art. I probably acted like a kid pointing out all the cool things in his studio. I was walking through my future dream.

I remember as a child, one of the cartoons I used to watch in the early morning was a cartoon called Jot. Jot and his friends were these little white circles with faces on them. They had hands and feet that didn't connect to their body. Each episode included a song. The arms and legs of these characters would disappear and the head would become a white ball which would bounce along the words, like karaoke for kids. He had original cels of Jot on the studio walls. I said, "Oh, I remember this."

Figure 9 - An original Jot cel given to me in my interview.

He replied, "Oh, I produced that show."

The first time I ever interviewed somebody and my subject had created a show I watched as a kid. It was absolutely incredible.

We walked into a large room at the end of the hall. On the far wall, I saw a device that intrigued me. It was around eight feet tall, four feet wide, and two or three feet deep. It featured lights at various positions pointing to a central platform.

I pointed said, "Wow, what a great rotoscoping machine"

He stopped. He looked over at me and said, "How do you know what that is?"

I replied, "Well, it has a pegbar and light table on top. You've got lights up above, so you need to see illuminate what's on the table. The pegbar is obviously for animation. You've got a 16 or 35 mm projector mounted underneath shining up from below to the translucent sheet under the pegbar. Obviously, you're filming people doing various actions and you're projecting it up to the animation disc and you're drawing over the projection. What else would it be? It's has to be a rotoscoping machine."

He looked at me, grinned and said, "I had that custom-designed and built for me. It's the only one of its kind. You took one glance and knew what it was." He stood there for a moment and smiled at me. "Do you want a job? Would you like to work for me?"

There I was, just over halfway through my college education, and I was offered a job doing exactly what I was studying to become.

By letting my excitement show during the interview and tour, and openly talking about things I liked and expressing myself, and showing him what I knew, he was drawn to my energy.

I didn't accept the job. I should have. Hindsight is 20/20. I should have taken that job, or at least gotten a summer internship. I never got back to him. Keeping in touch with him would have helped me tremendously as I started my career into animation.

What I learned was how to take every opportunity to advance myself. Even something simple like an English assignment can be used to make new connections or a future career. I also had a more enjoyable college experience than many people because I turned every assignment into something that interested me.

Even more important was the lesson that expressing interest was a good thing in any job interview. Staying calm, cool and collected can be seen as disinterested. But showing passion is what employers look for. I always let my passion show and it always works.

Once again, when I interviewed the owner of the studio I started at the top, and that always works well.

Chapter 7
Keller Williams is Calling

Keller Williams is the largest real estate company in the world. Back when my father, a seasoned Realtor, first started working with Keller Williams, they were relatively small.

My dad had been in real estate for quite a long time. Keller Williams worked differently than other realty companies. They offer profit sharing and a downline income from other agents. So, if you bring someone into the company, you get a percentage of their income, and people below them.

Profit participation is one of the strongest draws for Realtors. In addition to selling homes, you can make more money by bringing new Realtors into your downline.

When my dad first started with them, he was given a three-ring binder to use when pitching the profit-sharing concept to other potential Realtors. The same binder also helped train newcomers.

That was back in the early '90s and a lot of salesmen still used three-ring binders in sales pitches and presentations.

When Dad showed his pitch to me, I said, "You know, this is actually kind of boring. There's a much better way of presenting."

A couple years prior I had started giving a lot of public talks. I used a slide presenting software much like PowerPoint, but not PowerPoint. I told him, "Let me design something on the computer for you. "

Working with my father on the main selling points of the pitch, I created a better pitch and training program than the simple 3-ring binder. Dad would take my laptop to his meetings and return to give me notes.

To make the program even stronger, I added an entire section for Dad to use in his listing pitch to new potential home listing clients.

The new multi-purpose software worked well, and got even better as we worked to perfect it. The program was graphic, quick, it was much, much more impressive than a simple three ring binder.

That following summer we came up on the annual Keller Williams Conference. I figured the program worked so well for my father that other realtors would want to use it too. I paid for a small table at the conference and I presented my software. The reaction was mixed. Many Realtors at that time were not very computer savvy. My system was better than what they used, but many Realtors didn't want to invest in a laptop or learn how to use the simple software.

Figure 10 - My table at the Keller Williams convention where I sold my custom sales software.

But Keller Williams was a progressive company. They didn't follow, they led. Gary Keller, the co-founder of Keller Williams, came by my table and asked me to step him through my program. As I did, I explained my reasoning behind my choices and showcased the changes I made. I pitched him on how the software was faster and better than their printed materials. It was also cheaper to edit and replicate.

Gary understood what I had done and loved it. By the end of the conference he bought the full rights to my program along with a contract for me to update the software.

My first venture into original software development was a success and I sold it to what eventually became one of the largest real estate companies in the world.

I had created a better mouse trap. And then when I invested in marketing that idea at a national conference, the right person saw my idea.

If you want to succeed, you have to be willing to put in extra effort. I saw a better way and proved it.

I got lucky the Gary Keller came to my table. If someone else from Keller Williams had seen it and not liked it, they could have said no. But Gary's visit allowed me to start at the top.

Chapter 8
Well Hell, I Can Do That!

Sometimes inspiration comes from seeing others perform poorly.

When I was in high school and still running part of my father's construction company, I had started to design marketing materials for some of his vendors. I discovered that I really enjoyed advertising.

There was a small advertising company, Alter Advertising, I had seen when I was driving around town. I decided to stop in one day to see if I could do work for them. I asked to speak to the owner, who I found out was Fred Alter. He invited me into his office and I explained to Fred about how I had designed flyers and signs for some local companies. I pulled out my portfolio of samples and took him through it.

Fred looked at everything, leaned back in his office chair and said, "I'll tell you what. We can do anything here. If you find a guy who wants to put a tattoo on his pecker, we'll figure out how do it."

I liked him. He was pretty funny. He seemed to like me too. I was only 17 and he hired me. I wasn't hired to create designs, like I wanted, but he hired me as a salesman, commission only. So anything I sold I would earn a commission and if something fit within what I was capable of, I might be able to do some of the art and design on it too. I figured it was a good place to start and better than nothing.

Using some of my construction contacts, I pitched to a bunch of different people and started bringing in a lot of proposals for Fred to bid on. Every time I brought in a proposal, Fred looked at me shocked and said, "You got something else?"

"Yes," I replied, "and my clients are waiting for a bid."

I kept bringing proposals to Fred, but he never gave me any bids to take to my clients. It became clear that either he never expected me to actually do anything or if it was because he just couldn't manage his time very well. It bothered me because I had talked to these people and I had promised them I would get back to them with bids.

As I waited at Fred's agency, I'd listen to him on the phone and watch him work on one of his existing campaigns and put bids together for his other clients. That's when I realized that virtually everything he delivered to clients, was made by another company. He would just call other businesses who specialized in whatever he needed, got an estimate, marked it up and delivered it. I could do that!

After a few weeks of bringing in potential clients and Fred not helping me, I got frustrated. I walked out and took my clients with me.

Anything my clients needed, I found printers to create what they needed. I marked up my costs and added a fee for any design I provided.

I was finally able to follow up with my clients. Luckily, I landed every single deal. That was the beginning of Nomis Creations (SIMON backwards). It was a marketing company which I ran while in high school and used it to pay my way through college.

By watching what the owner of another business did and seeing his shortcomings, I learned how to run a marketing business. In this case, Fred's shortcoming was not getting back to me quickly enough.

I saw where he failed and said, "I can do that!" And then I went and did it.

You can say it all you want, but nothing happens without action.

Figure 11 - Here I am working on advertising in my home office while in high school.

Section 2
I am Mark – Hear Me Roar

I am not a shy person. At least I'm not shy in most situations.

As my kids grew up, they would complain, like all kids do, about how much studying they had to do. I told them I study more now than I ever did in school. Technology is expanding so fast, that you can never stop learning…or life, or a job, will leave you behind.

I've always known that I wanted to be an artist and tell stories. There's always new softwares to try, newer versions to learn… so I study, I practice, I do my own projects to prove to myself and others what I can do.

When I talk about what I can do, it's never a flight of fancy. It's always based on knowledge and experience. Experience, whether you get paid for it or not, gives you confidence. Confidence overcomes shyness.

If no one else would or could teach me I would teach myself. I would create my own projects and discover how to make use of all these new tools, and then I would talk about, and promote, what else I can do.

You can be the best in the world at what you do, but if no one knows it, they don't have the opportunity to hire you to do it.

So speak up.

Push yourself.

Try something new.

Build a skill.

Learn a trade.

And talk about it. In fact, roar about it.

Here's some examples of how speaking up helped me.

Chapter 9
The Power of Print

There are a lot of things in life you need to stand up for-- not only for yourself, but for what you believe in. And sometimes what you believe in changes the course of where you're going, and the actions that you take.

When I went to college at Stephen F. Austin State University - SFA - in East Texas, and I wanted to be the school cartoonist. There had been some really great cartoonists before me, including the cartoonist of the hit sports comic strip *Tank McNamara*, Bill Hinds, who has since become a friend of mine. He had left SFA a couple of years before me. During my freshman year the more recent editorial cartoonist at the school newspaper - called 'The Pine Log' – had left.

Figure 12 - I'm on the left standing with Bill Hinds, former cartoonists at SFASU.

Before I approached the *Pine Log*, I pulled together samples of other cartoons I had drawn. While I was in high school I was the school cartoonist, but more importantly, I had sold some editorial cartoons to the *Houston Post* as a freelancer.

I had also drawn a comic strip for a local paper in NW Houston. The strip was called *Dad's Place* and it was based on my flirtatious father. It was a good example of my cartooning, but I knew that *Dad's Place* was not a good fit for a college paper. I had to think of another cartoon to pitch.

Living in the dorm was the first time I had ever had a roommate, but I had heard lots of horror stories of crazy roommates. So I created about ten sample strips of a strip I called *Roomies*. The characters were a collection of opposites that did not attract. For instance, I had a kid who was scared of everything rooming with a kid who turned into a werewolf.

Figure 13 - My comic strip, Roomies, which ran in the school paper.

So, with my portfolio of editorial cartoons and comic strips I visited the Pine Log at the beginning of my freshman year. I told them there were two jobs I was interested in. One, I wanted to be the new editorial cartoonist for the school paper. And two, I wanted to do a comic strip, one or two strips every time the paper came out and the paper came out twice a week. I showed them my samples to prove I could do it. They said 'yes' to both ideas and they hired me on the spot. I was one of the first people in the history of the school to become the editorial cartoonist as a freshman. And few, if any, had drawn both editorial cartoons and a comic strip at the same time.

One of the things I enjoyed most about editorial cartooning was really finding the key issue within anything that was going on. And I was dealing with cartoons, anything from local, to the school, to national stories.

Figure 14 - SFASU's Pine Log student paper

The editorial staff didn't really give me a whole lot of rules I had to stick by, other than there were times where they'd have a very strong editorial column and wanted me to try and create a cartoon that went along with it. I drew cartoons at SFA for years. I had a great time doing it and they were pretty popular.

Figure 15 - My editorial cartoons for the Pine Log, our college paper.

One issue of *The Pine Log* included an editorial written by a friend of mine, Patty, about racism at the school. We were in the deep south, in East Texas, there was definite racism around. It was a subject I felt very strongly about. My mother was a racist and it drove me absolutely freaking nuts; I couldn't stand it. So I fought against that type of thinking whenever I had a chance.

I was free to draw editorial cartoons about almost

anything I wanted, and doing an editorial based on racism, or against racism because of Patty's article, was a perfect opportunity. I really got into it. I hit the subject pretty hard. My editorial cartoon was against the KKK - the Ku Klux Klan. Later that week, I did another cartoon for the same issue of the *Pine Log* – this time about how people felt about gays, because a lot of people were against gays in Texas. Surprise, surprise. I drew a cartoon that centered around Boy George. Boy George was a really popular pop singer, who was also gay, in the early/mid '80s. I did one about him being gay. I don't care if someone's gay, straight, or black, white, yellow, purple, it doesn't matter. What does bother me is how other people bully and segregate against people who seem to be different than them.

Figure 16 - The cartoons I drew for the school paper which they refused to print.

The *Pine Log* declined to run either cartoon. They declined to run the racism cartoon about the Ku Klutz Klan because one of the national offices of the KKK was 20 miles south of my school. The school paper was afraid. They were afraid of retribution. They were afraid of people calling them. They were afraid of threats.

My response was, "Good! Let people threaten. Let's bring this to the forefront. Let's talk about it. Let's get people talking about this. Let's get people to see who is on which side of this issue. I think it's fantastic! It's great press for the paper too." They wouldn't do it.

And they wouldn't run the gay cartoon, because they thought it was too defamatory. I fought tooth and nail with them about both cartoons, and they wouldn't run them. I didn't agree with their reasons.

I quit the paper. I didn't quit the paper just to make a statement, because that wouldn't have helped anybody; that wouldn't have done anything. I quit the paper and started my own competing paper. I wanted people to see the cartoons. I was going to run those editorial cartoons and I was going to make the statement my school was too scared to make.

Another friend mine at the *Pine Log*, Scott Miller, was also thinking about quitting in the school paper. I talked to him about what I was doing and pitched him my idea. He loved it. Scott quit the *Pine Log* and became my partner to publish our own paper to compete with the school newspaper.

Figure 17 - I'm on the right standing with my Belligerent Beacon co-publisher, Scott Miller (left) with rock star Joe King Carrasco in a behind-the-scenes photo.

We decided to be pretty belligerent and funny. We were going to talk about things the school paper was too afraid to. We were going to run more art. We were going to run poetry. We were going to have fun, and we were going to give a hardcore look at things and have the attitude of college students. We decided to call it the *Belligerent Beacon*.

Figure 18 - I published The Belligerent Beacon at SFASU.

We had a blast putting the *Belligerent Beacon* together, but we also knew it was going to cost us money. That was in the days before desktop computers, and long before laptops and design software. So, we had to hire the local city newspaper to do our type-setting for us, and then we needed them to print the *Belligerent Beacon* for us as well. So we needed to raise money. In addition to covering our costs, we also wanted to make a profit for our work.

Originally, we were thinking we were just going to do a two or maybe four-page quick little thing just to kind of get some stuff out just to prove our point and sell a little advertising on it.

Let me back up here for a moment. When I was in high school I had started a small advertising agency called Nomis Creations (Simon backwards). I continued to create advertising for clients in Houston and around my college town of Nacogdoches. That's how I paid my way through school. I had experience creating and selling advertising.

The Pine Log advertising sales materials were pitiful. I knew I could do better. I took what the school had been doing to sell ads and I revamped it. I designed our sales materials the way I thought they should work.

We created our own ad campaign and marketing materials and Scott and I went out and sold advertising. Our sales pitch and sales materials worked. We sold quite a bit of advertising - so much so that our little one-sheet ended up being a 12 page first-edition - as big as the school paper.

We ended up taking a lot of the advertising clients from the school paper because we presented better materials. The editors at the *Pine Log* were mad at us but there's nothing they could do about it.

We came out strong with our first issue. We had a lot of different articles, but one of the main things I wanted was to print those two editorial cartoons that the school wouldn't print. In the feature article we explained why the school wouldn't print them due to fear of violence and we explained that we weren't afraid to stand up for what was right.

You know what happened? Absolutely nothing. No one came out against us. In fact, people loved it; they thought it was great. Writers and artists wanted to submit their work to us. We received more content and we got more advertisers. We started to make more money.

Then, the school revamped their entire marketing campaign. They copied all of our materials because we were selling more ads than they were. The school paper actually ended up improving as a result of our starting the *Belligerent Beacon* as well.

We sent a few copies of the *Belligerent Beacon* to friends

at other schools in Texas. They liked it and wanted our paper, so we ended up getting distribution through four different universities – Stephen F. Austin State University, Baylor, University of Texas - UT, and Texas A&M.

We had come out strong with our attitude of being belligerent, but we needed something else to be belligerent about.

Then something else caught our attention. The student government at SFA really seemed like it was a bunch of bullshit, and the guy who was current president, Steve Payne, seemed like he was full of shit. We didn't like him at all. We didn't like his attitude. We didn't like the fact that nothing was happening to help the students. It seemed like he was using the position just to make himself look like a big guy. So we decided to take Steve down.

The *Belligerent Beacon* editorial staff (me and Scott) decided to sponsor somebody to run against Steve for Student Government president. But we knew it couldn't be a normal person. We needed someone different. Someone visually striking and someone we could mold into an ideal candidate to make a statement about the ridiculous student government.

Scott and I had a friend named Terry Spies (pronounced Spees). Terry was the king of the nerds of the school. He was a super nice guy and he knew he came across as a nerd. We didn't tease him about it, but we didn't hide the fact either. Terry must have been 6'-4" or 6'-5". He was really skinny, and sported coke-bottle thick rim glasses. He carried a briefcase instead of a backpack. He'd literally wore a pocket protector in his shirt pocket. If you can imagine a nerd, Terry looked like a bigger nerd.

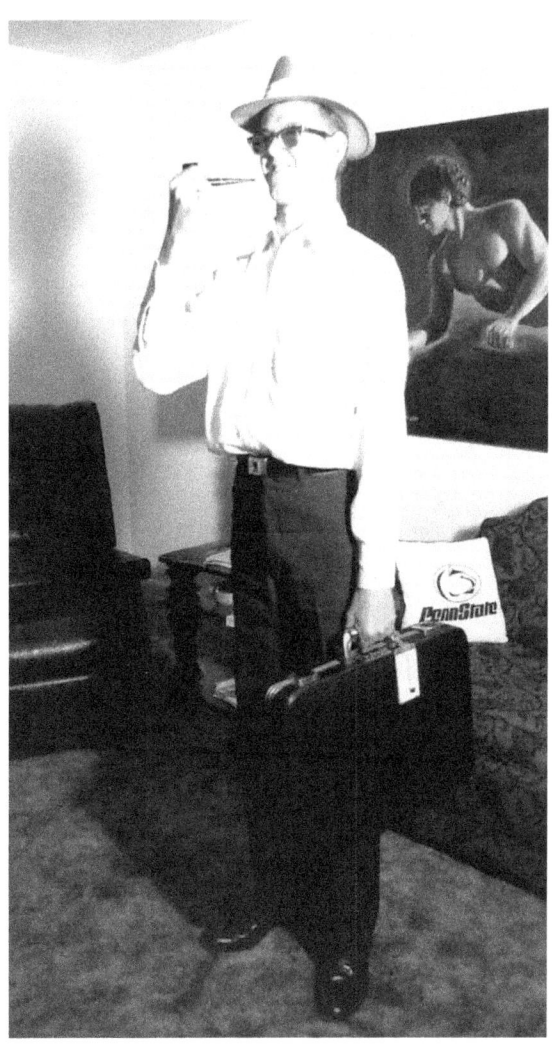

Figure 19 - Terry Spies, proud hero. One of the promotional photos I took of him for our student council campaign.

So we figured we would run Terry for student government president. We pitched him the idea that we're going to turn him into a superhero - sword in one hand and his briefcase in the other. We'd have him surrounded by gorgeous co-eds hanging onto him, and we were going do a series of comic strips about him that we would release every couple of days to make them collectibles across campus.

Figure 20 - The flyers we designed for our odd campaign to run Terry for student govt. president.

Then we planned to produce full page ads for him in our paper. And we would have him battling bad guys. Every super hero needs a super villain so we decided to have him battle Dr. Spamwad.

Figure 21 - Poster for the campaign.

Spamwad was an alliteration. We never told anybody this, or at least we never put it into writing. We didn't want anyone to be able to prove who Dr. Spamwad was. SPAMWAD stood for Steve Payne, A Man Without A Dick. We told a few people so they could tell other people, and it went verbal viral before the internet existed, but no one could prove it (meaning: no one could blame us). In fact, this is the first time Dr. Spamwad has been outed in print.

Terry quickly became one of the most popular people on campus. The guy who couldn't get a date to save his life all of a sudden had girls all around him all the time.

Terry didn't win the election, but he alone got more votes in that election than the entire previous election's total votes combined. In fact, the election that we ran Terry in got more than three times as many votes as they had ever gotten on campus. We got people to get off their butts and vote. We got them to pay attention to what was going on, and we did it while having fun with the whole situation. And we showcased and profiled important school subjects that we thought weren't handled properly. We were the print version of the *Daily Show* before the *Daily Show* existed.

So be willing to stand up for what you believe in. Be willing to take a chance. Be willing to piss off half of all people. It's amazing what can happen. Things can grow bigger than you expect, and you can end up touching a lot more people than you ever thought possible.

Chapter 10
Is It Bragging or Self Promotion?

You have to be willing to brag about your accomplishments to move ahead. I've never understood why people think bragging is a bad thing. OK, maybe bragging is a bad word to use. But talking about what you've accomplished is the best way to get more gigs and promotions.

There's a way to talk about your accomplishments and a way not to do it. But when you've done something special, people should know about it. Or if you've done something and someone else has taken credit for it, you need to correct that situation and let everyone know the truth.

If people don't know what you have completed, you hurt yourself and your future opportunities. And you're hurting others because everyone needs help at times, and if people don't know what you can do, they don't know you can help them.

When I was 14, I worked for my father's construction company - Simon Corporation - in North Houston. We built large custom homes. Dad would wake me up in the morning and we would go over a list of what needed to be done for the day. He would drive me to the job sites and drop me off.

Figure 22 - Working on a jobsite at a young age with my dad, Ted Simon.

Then, Dad hired Rick to be our superintendent. Rick ran the construction jobs for us.

Rick and his family were living in one of the unsold homes we built. He would stay in one of our vacant homes with his family until it sold.

Dad would drop me off with Rick and go over what needed to be done during the day. Dad would leave and take care of his office and design work. Rick would drop me off at the various job sites with all the tools I needed. I would do all the work. At the end of each day Dad would either come get me or Rick would drop me off at home. I worked like this under Rick for a number of months.

One night I was having dinner with my family. It was just the three of us, my mom, my dad and me. I was the only child. Dad talked about how great Rick was doing; how happy our clients were; how the jobsites were running smoothly; how all the repairs were getting done right the first time. And Mom happily said, "Well, this is great. This is what we've been looking for."

I was listening to all of this and I was thinking that

every example Dad mentioned was something I had done. Rick hadn't done any of it. So I sat there, wondering if I should say something. There I was, a 14 year old boy and there was this shmuck in his 30's getting credit for all my hard work.

I thought, "This isn't right!" I spoke up and said, "Dad, Rick didn't do any of that."

He replied, "What do you mean? Everything is getting done."

"Yeah," I said. "It is getting done, because I'm the one doing it."

"What do you mean?" Dad asked.

I said, "When you drop me off, Rick just takes me over to the job sites, drops me off and he goes back home and stays with his kid in the house while his wife goes out shopping. I'm doing all the work. I'm the one dealing with all your clients, ask them."

It felt weird at first to say all this and contradict what they thought of Rick, but I was proud of the work I had done. I deserved the credit. If I was sweeping a gutter, I made sure it was perfectly clean. If I was doing a repair, I wanted that repair to be seamless. I took pride in every single thing I did and I did it the best I could. There was no job above or below me. I was doing what I was told to do and it showed in the results.

Mom looked at my dad at dinner and said, "Ted, why are we paying Rick if Mark is doing all the work?"

Dad replied, "I don't know. I'll have to look into it." He was quiet during the rest of dinner. I could see he was hard in thought.

Figure 233 - Signs I designed and printed for our company.

The next few days Dad spoke with a few of our clients to confirm who was doing the work. They all told him I was the only person they ever saw working on their homes and that I did all the repairs.

Then he spoke to Rick. Rick took all the credit for himself. And then Dad fired him and gave me the job as superintendent. All of sudden I was 14 and I was superintendent of a custom home building company.

My schedule was crazy, but I enjoyed it. I was still in middle school. Dad gave me a pickup truck to use for work. It was an old '67 Chevy. It was a blue stick shift classic. I didn't have a driver's license yet, so I had to be careful when I drove to the job sites. During the school year I would drive out to the job sites in the morning to get the jobs going, check with our clients, and check with our workers. Then I would drive to my middle school, Wunderlich Middle, and I would park in the teacher's lot. There was no other parking lot since no other kids could drive. After school I would drive back to the job sites, close down the day, do whatever repairs needed to be done and then drive home for dinner. I did this for years.

When I turned 15 I got a worker's driving permit, which allowed me to drive a year before I was old enough to get a full license. They called it a hardship permit, but it was hardly a hardship. I never got a ticket and never got in trouble for driving.

Figure 24- My work truck in front of one of our homes under construction.

The point is, I got a raise and a promotion to superintendent because I was willing to stand up for what I had done and I didn't let someone else take credit for my work. You don't have to put someone down to stand up for yourself, but you need to stand up and speak up.

Remember, you can be the greatest at what you do, but if no one knows it, you're not giving them the opportunity to hire you or work with you.

Chapter 11
Why Have Lots of Job Interviews When You Can Start At The Top?

The most accepted process to get a job is thought to be to speak with someone in Human Resources, HR, or a manager and then have a series of interviews with people of increasingly important roles at the company.

The problems with this approach are two-fold. One, it can take a lot of time. Two, this gives a lot of people the opportunity to say 'No' and end your chance to land that job.

I prefer to start with the top person, the person who makes the final decision at a company. If the top person wants you, no one else would dare say 'No' about hiring you.

Immediately after I graduated college, I thought working in Hollywood sounded pretty cool.

I love movies. I love TV. I had been in theater in high school and the film department college and thought, "Why not give Hollywood a shot?"

So within two weeks of graduating, I shut down the advertising company I owned, sold my house and I moved to Los Angeles. I didn't know anyone in LA. I had never been to LA. It was a risk like most big changes in life. If you want to succeed, you've got to be willing to take a risk.

My family didn't have any entertainment industry connections whatsoever. What I had was a knowledge of theater and I knew how to design and swing a hammer because of my background building homes with my dad.

I thought my knowledge of construction would be my easiest way into the entertainment industry. I knew how to design and build houses, but I didn't know how film and TV sets were built. I knew theater. But in theater the flats are fabric covered. It's completely different on a film set.

So I figured, "If I want to learn how to design and build sets, I should learn from the best." I researched and found a company called Serrurier and Associates, the largest set building company in Los Angeles at that time, in the mid-80s. They were based in Pasadena in the East side of the valley.

Rather than just calling or sending a letter –there was no such thing as e-mail or the internet back then - I got in my car and drove to their facility. When I walked in I asked to speak to the owner and namesake, Steve Serrurier.

To start at the top, it often means starting with the person at the top of any situation or company. So I went straight to the owner of the company, Steve. I didn't have any connections to him, but it's amazing what can happen when you simply ask for what, or who, you want.

I wanted to meet Steve. I asked for him and got lucky, he was available. Steve brought me back to his office and I had a portfolio with me of my theater designs and house plans I had drawn up. I also had photos of the custom homes we had built. The size of our homes were up to 10,000 square feet and were quite impressive.

Figure 25- A photo I showed to Steve of a kitchen we built in one of our homes.

The reason I brought in those photos was to prove I knew construction even though I may not have known the specifics of set building. I was very direct about what I did and didn't know. I knew construction, and I had a passion for design and building. I proved to the owner that I understood what it took to design, and how to build, how to swing a hammer, how to cut, all the various talents he was likely to need in his shop.

He hired me right then. I started the next day.

Starting with the top person at the company gave me a very quick entry into working in the industry. The owner of the company recognized the value of my relevant skills and how it would help his company, whereas someone with less knowledge of the industry, such as an HR person, might have dismissed my skills as being too different. I didn't give anyone else the chance to tell me "No."

Figure 26 - Elephant prop we built at Serrurier & Associates.

Chapter 12
Nickelodeon Needs Me

When my wife and I first decided to move from Los Angeles to Orlando, we learned a great lesson in how to land a job that you want. The biggest part of that lesson was not to listen to Human Resources.

After the big earthquake in San Francisco in October of 1989, my wife, Jeanne, and I decided to move out of California to Orlando. Orlando had warm weather and the entertainment industry was just building up as a great place to produce. Disney had just opened up the Disney/MGM studios, which functioned as both a theme park and a shooting studio. Universal was also building both a theme park and sound stages which had not yet opened. The word in the entertainment industry was Orlando was about to become Hollywood East, so it sounded like a perfect place for us.

When we got to Orlando we discovered that Nickelodeon was about to open on the Universal Studios Florida backlot. The network had recently gone national and they were about to open up two dedicated sound stages at Universal so they could have guaranteed and free audiences at any time for their popular game shows like *Double Dare*.

It sounded like it would be a lot of fun to work there and we thought with all of our Hollywood production credits it would be easy to land jobs at the Nickelodeon's Orlando studios. Nickelodeon was an entire network. That meant a lot of staffing. How many people in Orlando in 1989 could have our West Coast credits?

Once we settled into Orlando, we tried to get into the Nick offices but they were behind the gates of Universal and we didn't have access to enter.

We found a phone number for Nickelodeon and called them up. Jeanne was production coordinator at the time and I was an art director, and we inquired about who we should talk to about getting jobs. We were told, "Send your resumes to Human Resources," The person on the phone gave us a Nickelodeon address on Universal property. We replied, "Okay." At that point we had no reason not to believe them.

We sent in our cover letters and resumes and thought, "This is great! They are going to call us any day and we'll get the jobs we want." We waited. And we waited some more. We never got the call.

While we anxiously awaited the call, we kept working. As a freelancer you never stop looking for work. So, while waiting for that inevitable Nickelodeon call, I started working on some commercials for a local production company. Jeanne was doing other work in the industry.

After we hadn't heard anything for a long while, we called Nickelodeon again, got someone else on the phone. We asked the same question, "Hi, we've got LA experience as an art director (or as a production manager when Jeanne called). We are here in town and would love to talk to you guys about getting work there. Who should we talk to?"

The guy on the phone responded, "Well, send it to this person in Human Resources at Nickelodeon."

So we shrugged and sent in our second set of resumes. We thought, "Oh, this is it. We're definitely getting in this time. They're going to see our resumes now." And then, nothing. We waited for a few weeks. Nothing. No response at all.

After a few more weeks we tried again. We called the Nickelodeon studios again and were told the same thing. Human Resources. We sent in a third set of cover letters and resumes. Resumes with strong Hollywood credits.

We still got no response. We thought, "What's going on? How could there possibly be so many people in Orlando with all of our experience that we don't even get a call?" It's one thing once you interview with someone and don't get hired, I get that. But to not even get called in for an interview with our experience? That baffled us.

In the meantime, we had been working on commercials and Jeanne had been meeting a lot of industry people. A few weeks after we sent in our third set of resumes, Jeanne had a meeting with executive producer Debra Cibella at Century III, a post-production facility located on the Universal lot. Debra met with Jeanne one afternoon. She told Jeanne she wasn't hiring at that time, but she liked to know who was available for when various gigs came up.

Jeanne showed Debra a huge production board for a feature film she'd done as practice for breaking down a script. Jeanne had been a coordinator in Los Angeles and wanted to move up to production management in Orlando. So to prove how organized she was, she did a complete production board and breakdown. For anyone who may not understand a production board, it breaks down every scene of a script into colored strips that represent day or night, location, actors, props, and then organizes them into a shooting schedule with all the information you need to completely schedule a production. There's a thousand things you have to keep in mind for scheduling any production. To prove she could do it, she did it.

Figure 27- Promotional photo of Jeanne with her sample production board.

Debra was really impressed. She said, "This is all great. Obviously, you really know what you're doing." They shook hands and went their separate ways.

It wasn't long after that meeting when Debra had lunch with Nickelodeon's VP of production management, Loren

Gray. During lunch Loren started complaining that she couldn't find any good production managers in town. Debra smiled and told her, "Well, I just met someone who would be perfect for you, and she's got LA experience. She really knows how to organize. She's great."

Out of the blue, or so we thought, Jeanne got a phone call from Nickelodeon to go in for an interview. We thought, "Wow, someone finally saw one of our resumes."

Jeanne went in for her interview with Loren the next day. It seemed to be going great. They shared production stories. Jeanne showcased her sample production board and Loren was impressed. Then Loren looked at Jeanne and said, "I just have one concern and that's if you've got all this experience, why haven't you contacted us?"

Jeanne was shocked. She replied, "What do you mean why haven't I contacted you? If you didn't see my resume, how did you get my info?"

Loren told Jeanne about her meeting with Debra and Jeanne replied, "Oh. Well I actually had reached out to you. Many times. In fact I sent you three sets of resumes."

Loren replied, "What do you mean you sent three resumes? When and to whom?"

Jeanne told her the story of how we had called and were told to send our resumes in to Human Resources.

Loren got a really angry look on her face and stormed out of the room and said, "Stay here, I'll be right back."

She walked down to Human Resources and firmly stated, "I'm interviewing someone for a position I've been looking to fill for months and she said she's been sending us resumes for months yet I haven't seen anything. What are you doing down here?"

They evidently told Loren they were receiving resumes and just filing them. The problem was Loren and other department heads never looked in the Human Resource files. After spending years in the industry we've realized no one ever goes to Human Resources and asks them for resumes because Human Resources generally doesn't know anything about production. Producers and production managers know about production and what they look for in each position. Incoming resumes and information should have been forwarded to them, but it wasn't. That was a big lesson for us.

Loren returned to her meeting with Jeanne and looked at Jeanne and said, "Look, you're great. Sorry about the mix up and I'm so sorry it took us so long, but we finally found each other. Can you start next Monday?"

Jeanne said, "Absolutely, that would be fantastic." She got hired immediately as a production manager at Nickelodeon.

Jeanne got up and when she was about to leave she turned and said, "Oh, by the way, my husband's an LA art director. He was also reaching out to Nickelodeon."

Loren looked up at her and said, "What? Wait, stop. Come back, have a seat." She wrote down a phone number, handed it to Jeanne and said, "Call your husband and give him this phone number and tell him to call Charles in the art department now. Not later today, not tomorrow. Right now. We are in desperate need of art directors."

So Jeanne called me from Loren's office and told me a brief version of the story. I got off the phone and called the Nickelodeon art department immediately and spoke to Charles.

He said, "Oh my god, thank you so much for contacting us." He brought me in for an interview the next day. I was also hired in my first meeting and started working the week after Jeanne.

Again, it only took one interview to land the job, and I became the second art director at the new Nickelodeon Orlando studios.

3/31/93

Mark Simon

ART DEPARTMENT

Figure 28 - My studio ID at Nickelodeon.

So, what we learned from that experience was that if you want a job in any specialized position, do not go through Human Resources. They are not the ones who make the decisions. They're the ones who fill out the paperwork.

You see, people hire people they know and trust. So, your job search must be to get people to know you. That means getting involved in whatever industry you work in. For instance, you should help out at industry events, talk to people, sign people in at the registration tables, or volunteer to help. Anything you can do to meet people in your industry.

You know who runs industry (any industry) events? Successful people in that industry. Why are they successful? Because they know everybody. Why do they know everybody? Because they're involved. It's amazing how the cycle of business works.

Here's how most people and businesses hire.

First, you try to hire someone that you know and trust. You don't usually look for the absolute best person. You want someone you know can do the job and who you trust can do the job because it's your butt on the line. You usually have to fill open production positions quickly, so we call our first choice first, second choice second, and so on. The first person to accept gets the gig.

Second, if you can't find anyone available who you

know and trust, then you go to someone who you know and trust and ask them who they know and trust. Ninety to ninety-five percent of all the people I hire, I will find them in the first two steps.

Third, if the first options don't work, then I go to the resumes and portfolios I saved from people who send me samples.

If I still haven't found someone to hire, then I'll research in the industry trades or industry books. For instance, in the entertainment industry we have books and websites with listings of qualified people. Every industry has some sort of list or group or gathering. I'll then look there.

I virtually always find someone in one of those four ways. I have never once in my career of hiring people on over 4,500 productions asked anyone in a Human Resource department for any information whatsoever.

The only time I've ever had to place an ad was when I needed to hire an office assistant, which is not a highly specialized job.

On the flip side, few of the jobs I've landed have come from job listings. I can only remember one, and that was at the beginning of my career.

So if you are looking for a job and you look in the job listings and you don't see many available jobs, don't worry. Most jobs never get to the point of being posted.

Another lesson from this story, if you want a specific job, prove you can do it, even if you have never been paid to do that job.

Jeanne's having created a production board on her own, is a great example of how to prove you can do a job. Experience is experience, whether you get paid to do it or not.

After my Nickelodeon experience, I've never gone to anyone in Human Resources to find a job. I always go straight to the people who make the final decision in hiring. That means others who hire do the same thing. Do yourself a favor and avoid HR. Start at the top with the head of departments and business owners.

Chapter 13
Find a Hole and Fill It

Starting at the Top sometimes takes strategic thinking. One great way to land the job you want is to find a hole at a company and prove you can fill that hole.

I had a few reasons for wanting to write monthly articles for *Animation Magazine*. I love to write. I love to tell stories, I love information, and I love sharing information.

Animation Magazine is the biggest and the best animation industry magazine - one I had been reading for ten years and I really wanted to start writing articles at the top, to write for them.

Another reason is that writing articles for a major magazine is also a great PR. It lets everyone in the industry know who you are, what you're up to, what your knowledge-base is, and it becomes advertising. But writing articles is an instance when advertising pays you. I got paid to write the articles and I earned money again from the extra gigs. As long as you do a great job with the writing, this is a fantastic way of marketing yourself.

In order to land a job writing articles for *Animation Magazine*, I did some research. I had been reading it for years and saved them all so it was easy to research. I had to figure out what my angle would be for a series articles. What would I propose? I knew better then to just call and say, "Hey, I want to write for you." I had to have a plan. I had to offer them something, something that they weren't getting from anyone else.

One of the ways to get a job somewhere, or land a new client, is find a hole and fill it. So that's what I looked for. I looked for a hole in what they were providing with their magazine.

As I looked at the mast head for the magazine, it said 'The Business, Technology & Art of Animation and VFX'. Okay. So, I read through a number of issues to see how they fulfilled the promise of their mast head. There were a lot of articles about the art of animation, how 'people did this' and 'behind the scenes' of that, and 'here's what is coming out' about this movie, and 'here are the stars' from that movie, and 'this production just landed a deal'.

But, I realized, I didn't see anything about the business of animation. I didn't see any articles about what it took to work as a freelancer, how to market a small animation studio, and how things worked inside the animation industry.

I thought, "That's it. I'm going to propose an article or a series of articles about the business of animation."

Figure 29 - The masthead of Animation Magazine inspired my series of articles.

Then I sat and wrote down a number of ideas for articles. I needed to be prepared for when I called the magazine. I needed more than just a concept. I needed solid ideas for articles. I also needed a few really strong written examples. I had written articles for other periodicals, but I knew I needed samples to support my exact pitch.

Once I was happy with my overall concept, I wrote a few articles. Looking at their magazine articles as examples, I saw that most of their pieces were around 650 words. I wrote three sample articles of the right length and perfected them.

It was only then when I called the editor-in-chief of the magazine, Ramin Zahed. I went straight to the top, to the person who hires the writers.

I just called him up. It was easy. The phone number was right there in the magazine. I got Ramin on the phone and I introduced myself, "Hi. My name is Mark Simon. Do you have just a moment? I've got an idea for a series of articles that I would like to write for you, and I'd like to throw the idea off of you and see what you think."

Ramin replied, "Yeah. I've got just a moment. Sure. What are you thinking?"

I continued, "Look, I've been reading your magazine for years. I love the magazine. But I was looking at the mast head and I saw that it said 'the business, technology and art of animation. But I noticed that you don't have any articles that are truly about the business of animation. You've got articles about deals that are done but not actually the how-to of the business."

He replied, "Okay. So, what are you thinking?"

I said, "Well, I thought that I could do a series of articles called, *Mind Your Business*."

Then I gave him eight examples of the types of articles I would do. I suggested ideas like how to write a resume that would land you a job and a fun approach to how waiting by the phone for a job is like waiting by the phone for your girlfriend to call.

I pitched a fun approach to serious issues which would make my articles interesting to read. And he said, "You know what?" He said, "That sounds pretty good. Go ahead and write up what you just told me and send it to me, and I'll have our team take a look."

I outlined those eight brief ideas I had come up with, and I sent them to him with the best of the sample articles I had written. In less than a week, Ramin called me up and he said, " We love this idea. Let's get started right away and see how it goes and let's start a series of articles."

Figure 30 - One of my articles in Animation Magazine.

By doing my research and finding a hole and having a way to fill that hole, I was prepared for a perfect pitch. I didn't just say, "You've got a hole. I want to fill it." I said, "You've got a hole. Here's HOW I want to fill it." And I gave him examples.

I also made sure not to denigrate the magazine. I told him how much I liked it.

I've heard of other people making pitches and they start with how bad the company/magazine/network is and how they are the ones to save it. That never works out well.

I landed the job with one phone call at the top magazine in the industry. I wrote for them for many years. When I left that magazine, I instantly got picked up by another major magazine, *Animation World Network* (www.AWN.com), writing more of the same monthly articles. I wrote more than 100 animation business articles over a period of 10 years.

Potential clients read my articles and called me. I was asked to speak at conferences. I was asked to write for other magazines. When I called a studio, they usually knew who I was. It was by far the best promotion I ever could have gotten for myself and my business.

Chapter 14
Gave My Left Leg For a Black Belt

Not all of my statements have been from being loud and obnoxious. Some have been from pain and emotion. Letting your emotions coming out is not only just what you feel on the inside. But there are times, it has to do with what you feel on the outside. Other times, it's a mixture of both.

When my boys were very young, around six, I got them into martial arts. I had studied both Tae Kwon Do and Judo in high school and college and I wanted my boys to have that foundation.

Once I saw that they were going to stick with it, I joined them in training. I was in my early to mid-40s. I loved it. I love the training, the physicality and I loved the dedicated time I spent with my boys a few times every week. I set up their belt testing schedule so I tested with them for every belt.

We went through the ranks together. We trained two hours a day, three days a week and had fantastic time. We competed in state and national tournaments and we did fantastic. In fact, my boys are each three-time national champions and I am a two-time national champion in Tae Kwon Do.

Figure 31 - Our National Champion photos.

But the moment that stands out most in my mind, even more than the national championships, was when we tested to get our black belts.

Training for a black belt test is intense. It's a brutal four-hour physical test with tons of sparring and proving we knew more than ten complex forms. My boys and I worked hard, hard, hard.

We were in the dojo a week before the test, going through a grueling workout to make sure we were ready. We had been working out for about 45 minutes and I threw a right side kick - my left calf muscle snapped and I dropped to the ground in agony. The muscle just popped. I could feel it go. I swear, I heard it pop, and that was only one week before our test.

The pain was excruciating. I couldn't walk. I couldn't drive. I had to call my wife to come pick us up.

Testing for that black belt meant everything to me. First of all, I'd been training for it for years. But second of all, my boys had also been training for years and I wanted to test with them. I wanted us all to experience that huge moment in our lives...together.

The problem was, I couldn't even stand. The muscle completely seized on me. After it snapped, you could see a ball of muscle frozen under my calf. It looked deformed.

The week leading up to the test was painful. I continued to take the boys to class to train. Over a few days I was able to move my injured leg, but I couldn't walk normally or fully extend my injured leg. I stretched, balanced on one leg in each session and hopped through each form as well as I could. I did it all on one leg.

None of us knew what condition I would be in for the test. I kept painfully training with the expectation that I would be able to test.

On the Friday before the test, I was able to get around on one leg, but my left leg was useless. All it could do was help me balance.

The time came to make a decision on testing or not. I

couldn't give up. I looked at everyone in our dojo and declared, "I'm going for it."

My Sensei questioned me, "Are you certain? You can't walk and you could make it worse."

I nodded, "But I can hop. I know every part of the test. I know I can do it. Let's just tell the head of the association at the test what happened."

That's exactly what my Sensei did. The two people overseeing the test were the two highest ranked caucasians in the world. The highest ranked female in the world Master Brenda Sell - eighth-degree - and the highest ranked white male in the world, Master Sell - ninth-degree. She informed them that while I had one crippled leg, I would fight through the entire test with honor. They agreed to allow me to test.

We showed up at the testing facility the morning of the test. The knotted muscle in my calf had decided to wait until that moment to release and all the blood that was held in the torn muscle ran down inside my leg to form a painful dark bruise. My lower leg, ankle and foot were bright, bright purple. I could put my foot down on the ground, but it hurt like hell and looked even worse.

Figure 32 - I am third from the left, standing on one leg at our black belt test due to my injury.

Many parts of a black belt test can be done with your arms. However, there are parts that you can't just standing around and you have use both legs.

One of the hardest parts of the test was sparring against two other black belts at the same time. That's hard enough when you are healthy, but with one bum leg it's awful. As much as I tried not to use my bad leg, I did end up kicking with it and jumping off it. Each time I used my leg it was excruciating. They beat the crap out of me, but I never backed down, I never backed away, and I never stopped.

Then we had to perform ten different forms. A form is like a dance of specific martial arts moves as if you are fighting an invisible person. It's beauty in motion - except for me. I was not beautiful on that Saturday. But I was accurate.

The first hour of the test I was in absolute pain. The second hour was worse. By the third hour I was in tears. I tried as much as I could to stay on one foot, but there were times I just couldn't and I put everything I had into the test.

The testers asked me a few times how I was holding up, but they never took it easy on me. Nor did I ask them to.

I was also emotional. Through my pain and tears I was also watching my boys test. They were amazing. They looked like champions every step of the way. I was so proud!

My motions were welling up due to what I was going through. The pain was horrible. Tears streamed down my face. My body wanted to fall but I forced myself through.

When we got to the end of the test, we were all a sweaty mess and we lined up. I stood there, barely able to stand, next to my two boys and it was announced that all of us had passed.

I looked over at my boys with absolute pride. Everything they had accomplished to become black belts at such a young age.

I was in so much pain I fell over. I was also proud of myself. The heaving sobs leapt out of me. All the pain and emotion exploded at once.

Figure 33 - My boys and I celebrating our new Black Belts after I dropped to the floor.

Then the biggest surprise was announced. I was given a special accommodation because of the hardships that I pushed through in order still test and achieve my black belt on only one leg. I received one of the highest scores of the testing class, which also made my boys proud.

It was a moment I'll never forget. During the test, I let my emotions push me through because it was an incredibly difficult thing to do.

It was a great lesson for my kids to experience. If you really want something, don't let anything stop you. Let your emotions help carry you through the tough times. Showing emotions is not a weakness, using your emotions and allowing people to see what you're feeling is a sign of strength.

Section 3
Never Too Young

I was taught to respect my elders. But I quickly realized that just because someone is older, doesn't mean they deserve my respect, nor does being older mean you know better.

Don't get me wrong. Everyone deserves respect regardless of age...until their actions dictate otherwise.

I also believe in experience, but...

Not everyone learns from their experience.

Over the years I saw my own father get stepped on by older people in business situations because it was beaten (literally) into him by his father to respect all his elders. Because of this, some of his 'elders', who didn't deserve respect, took advantage of him.

I ran into ageism a few times growing up. Since I was so young and was running crews for my dad's construction company, some of the contractors didn't want to listen to me. Moments like that are a test for anyone. Will you back off or stand firm? If you are sure of yourself, stand firm.

An ass doesn't deserve respect, regardless of how old they are. Experience is only relevant when people learn from their mistakes and continually grow in knowledge and ability.

The following chapters share how I didn't let my age hold me back.

Chapter 15
Skateboarding – Public Nuisance or Business Opportunity?

I am a big believer that kids can do a lot more than most people give them credit for. One of the reasons I believe that is because of the passion I had as a kid for the things that I was into, and what I was able to do with that passion.

When I was 12, I was really into skateboarding. I picked it up quickly. I was always good at balance and eye-hand coordination sports. When I got into skateboarding, I instantly started winning contests. In fact, the only ones I didn't win were my first one, right after I'd started, and my last one. I took fourth place out of 12 in my first contest and I was hooked. I won first place in every other competition until I entered the largest skateboarding contest in Texas where I took third place in freestyle. I had a small amount of local fame from all my wins.

Figure 34 - When I was 12 years old practicing a stunt on one of my own skateboard designs.

Along with skateboarding, I also read skateboard magazines.

I read about really cool skateboard deck designs from California, but in Houston we didn't have the latest in equipment. But even the cool boards I saw pictures of didn't have some of the design elements I wanted to see in a skateboard.

One night at dinner I talked to my dad about what I had seen and what I'd like to have in a skateboard deck. He said to me, "Why don't you make your own?"

I thought about those simple words for a moment and said, "Okay. I'll make my own."

Dad taught me how to design a skateboard deck. Not that he knew anything about skateboards, but he knew how to design things so they'd be balanced in shape. I used what he taught me and I started to design my own line of skateboards that I planned to make for myself.

I made my first deck and it worked out really, really well. It was really cool.

Dad suggested I take my design to the next step, "You ought to name these." So, I came up with a name - Nomis Boards - which is Simon backwards. It was really cool. I kept working on other ideas for decks and ended up with six or seven different designs. I was ready to create more boards – better boards.

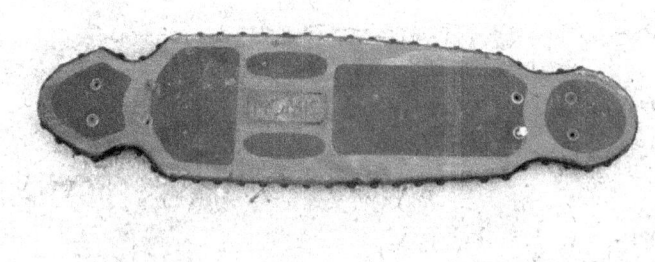

Figure 35 - The first test design of a Nomis Board.

Dad would take me to the lumber yard and we'd get raw lumber of either oak or ash. We had a large workshop at our house and I was raised using tools. Everything I needed was in our shop. I had access to anything and everything I needed to build the skateboard decks - and I did all of it myself.

Figure 36 - Our woodworking shop
next to our garage growing up.

About a mile from our house was a Schwinn bicycle store where I bought all of my local skateboarding equipment. They had all the trucks, and all the wheels, and the popular board decks - so I hung out there a lot.

Whenever I went to Schwinn to buy new supplies, I rode my new boards. The guys who owned and ran the Schwinn store started asking me about my boards. I told them about how I had designed and built them all.

They asked me, "How many do you have?"

I replied that I had about ten decks built.

They looked at each other, smiled, and looked back to be and said, "Well, how are you selling them?"

I shrugged, "I'm not."

They smiled bigger, "Do you want to?"

That conversation led Schwinn to become my distributor. It's funny thinking about it now, but my parents were never involved with any business dealings I had with Schwinn. I handled all of it myself. Dad had helped me understand what my costs were, including my own labor, so

I could make sure to earn a profit on each board. But I handled the entire affair myself.

Dad showed me how to create stickers so I could brand my boards. I used some of the stickers on my boards and laminated them into the decks. I used some other stickers on my other boards and my school folders.

On weekends and nights, I'd make my boards and then I would take them over to Schwinn and they would sell them. I brought in some of my extra stickers, and they sold them too.

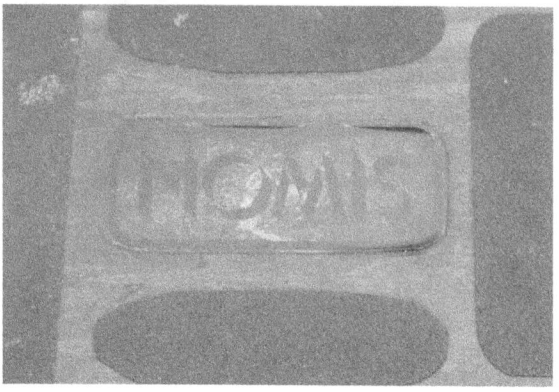

Figure 37 - One of my stickers mounted into one of my skateboard decks.

So, when I was 12, I had my own line of skateboards. Pretty heady shit for a pre-teen. I loved it. Can you imagine going to a skateboard park as a 12 year old, and kids you don't know come up to you and hold up their board and it has your sticker under it or they come up to you and they're riding one of your skateboards? I'm sure I was hard to live with for a while.

So if you want your kid to succeed and want to inspire them to start at the top, allow them to pursue anything they are interested in. They could be more capable than what you could give them credit for. If my dad hadn't suggested that I create my own skateboards to see if I really did have a better idea, I wouldn't have had the opportunity to create my own line of skateboards.

I'm far from alone in having some success as a kid. There are a lot of really talented kids out there doing incredible things. There are even more kids who could succeed beyond their dreams if they only had the support to try.

Opportunity and support are probably the two biggest things that you can do for somebody, and that set me on my path of always starting at the top. When you succeed, even with minor success, as a kid, you discover what you are capable of. And that attitude of knowing you can do anything and believing in yourself makes you completely unstoppable as you move through life.

Chapter 16
VP at 14 – Why Not?

When I was 14, I was vice president of a custom home building company. That probably sounds a lot more impressive than it really was at the time. My father started and owned Simon Corporation, which built large custom homes in northwest Houston. He was the president. He put me in as vice president because he needed the role filled and wanted to keep it in the family. My mom was secretary/treasurer. She oversaw the books and did the interior design.

Was I the right person to be vice president? Hell, no. But it allowed Dad to keep control in the family, and he used it as training for me. I was heavily involved in the business, but I wasn't making major decisions right away. However, he did teach me all about the bookkeeping. Everything was open to me.

Figure 38 - Simon Corp. offices

There I was. Just fourteen years old. I already understood double-entry bookkeeping. I understood marketing. I understood how to run crews. As I mentioned in another chapter, it wasn't long after that when I also became superintendent.

One of the biggest benefits of my not-so-earned job title was a giant ego boost. As a young teenager and vice-president of a company, it felt great.

We've all heard stories of people who turned down help from their family because they wanted to make it on their own. It's great to make it on your own, but why would you turn down something that will help you be successful?

Think about how much this helped me, to have on my resume when I go out in the world that I had been vice-president of a company. I never included how old I was on my resume, but to be able to put on there that I have been a vice-president was invaluable.

Figure 39 - A Simon Corp house under construction.
My work truck shown in front.

My corporate position also allowed me access to other things. Contacts. The connections that I made also helped me launch my advertising company a few years later. Any way you can give yourself or your kids self-confidence helps greatly in life. That's one of the greatest gifts my dad gave me was confidence and support. My position was more than just a title. It was training to start at the top.

Chapter 17
I Named The Houston Art Center

Back in 1983, when I was just 19 years old, I was approached by a woman who lived in our area, Alice Flores, to do some design work for her. She reached out to me because the local paper had written a story about the cartoons and art I had created.

Alice was on the board of a proposed art and theater complex to be built in downtown Houston, Texas. They needed a name and a logo for the complex as donations were coming in and they were starting on designs. She asked me if I could help them.

Like all good entrepreneurs I said, "Yes."

At first, she tried to pull the same routine on me that all artists hear, "We don't have any money put aside for this, but it would be great for your resume." For the record, they raised over $66 million for that complex.

I was young but not stupid. I told her how much I would charge for the logo design. We negotiated back and forth and settled on an amount.

I was the nerd artist who actually read books on art licensing and law. I knew the standard deal for large design agencies when they create logo design. But I was not a large agency. Knowing the industry standards seemed to make her deal with me more as an equal than as a kid. Knowledge helps.

The following week we got together to go over my initial ideas. I told her I thought it would be great to call the facility The Center. For marketing their events and shows, it was great. They could say "Be in the Center of the Arts."

She liked that idea, but wasn't totally sold.

Then I added, "It's also a great name that can be easily adjusted when you get a large donor. You can name it after them. It can become 'The Smith Center' or 'The Alice Flores Center'. She loved the idea, so I was off to the design phase.

A few weeks later we met again and I presented her with a few designs, including the ones below.

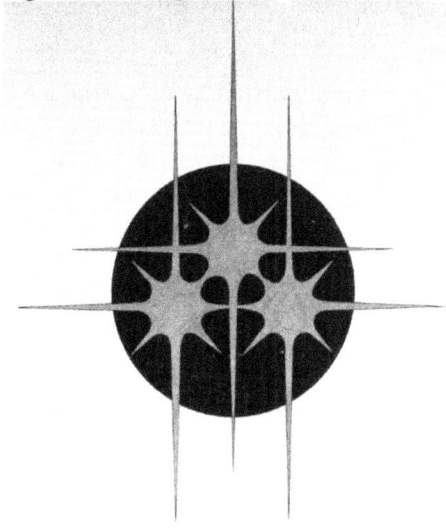

Figure 40 - The logo and name for Houston's Wortham Center which I created while still in College in 1984.

To grease the wheel, I used Alice's name as the example when I added a surname to the Center. Any time you can make someone feel special, it helps close a sale. It worked like a charm. She absolutely loved it.

She took my logo designs to the board and they chose the logo above to use for The Center. For decades, you could see the influence of my original design to the logos they used.

And sure enough, they got their whale of a donor and the name of the arts and theater facility became known as The Wortham Center, the same name that it currently holds. It is still the premiere theater facility in Houston.

Figure 41 - Wortham Center in Houston, Texas.

I may not have gotten everything I asked for in my negotiations, but I was happy with my deal and I was able to use that credit to get other work, while I was still in college. I landed a lot of promotion for my work on such a notable project at such a young age.

Don't let age stop you from acting professionally and asking for everything a more seasoned person would ask for.

Chapter 18
A Photo is Worth
An Unexpected Award

I had an unexpected beginning into professional photography.

I always loved cameras and I loved taking pictures. It's another visual form of storytelling which is the basis of everything I do.

When I was younger, my uncle gave me his 35 millimeter camera which didn't work. I took it apart and put it back together, and I got it to work. That started my fascination with cameras. But my entry into professional photography was a complete accident.

When I was in college in Nacogdoches, Texas, I was the school cartoonist for the school newspaper, The Pine Log. I drew the editorial cartoons and a weekly comic strip. And because of the I did for them I had a press ID, often called a Press Pass.

A Press ID can get you into places most people can't get. Now you wouldn't necessarily think that a cartoonist press pass would get you into many places, but the great thing about this world is people don't read the details. They definitely don't read the fine print.

One day, I was driving home after my college classes and saw a giant plume of black smoke on the horizon. And like every other red-blooded male in the country, I love fire. I'm definitely a pyromaniac. We're all pyros. I wanted to see the fire below the smoke so I drove towards the huge plume. When I saw some fire engines rushing down the road, I followed them.

I drove down a road on the outskirts of town as I saw two fire engines pull through a police road block on their way to a factory fire.

As I approached the roadblock, I pulled out my press ID. I drove up to the cops and I showed it to them. They took a quick glance at it and sure enough, they waived me through. My cartoonist press ID got me into a secure area.

I hopped out of my truck and ran over to the edge of the parking lot facing the burning building. It was a big paper factory that was on fire.

I saw a sign out front which said, "Over one million man-hours logged without a time lost accident."

I thought, "Now, that's some fantastic irony." I got down on one knee, and I started to line up my shot with that sign in the foreground and the burning factory on the background. Firemen were running up to it and they were dragging hoses behind them. There were fire engines all over the place.

My fore finger hovered above the shutter on the camera just as part of the plant exploded in front of me. The shock wave knocked me flat on my ass. What I didn't realize at the time was that when it knocked me back, my finger hit the shutter. When I went back to the school paper, I asked them to process the film.

When I took a look at all the photos, there was one photo I didn't realize I had taken of that explosion when I got knocked backwards. In that photo, you could see the 'time lost accident' sign in the foreground. In the background, there was a horizontal plume of smoke where the doors had been blown off. Two firemen were in the air and enveloped by smoke. They were lifted off the ground. It was an amazing photo.

Figure 42 - This is the only copy of the photo I can find.
Unfortunately the left and right sides of the picture are cut off.

The school paper ran the photo and they paid me for it. I didn't think anything else about it.

About four months later as I delivered my weekly comics to the paper and they handed me a wrapped package. I asked, "What is this?"

They replied, "Congratulations."

I asked what for.

They told me, "Your photo won an award."

"What photo?" It was four months after I had taken the photo and didn't connect the dots. I didn't know what they were talking about.

They explained it was for my explosion photo. They had forgotten to tell me they had even submitted it into a photo news journalism competition. "You won."

Figure 43 - The award I won for the accidental photo.

My first professional photo won a regional award for best photo news journalism. And it was a photo I took by accident. Sometimes sneaking into places that you're not supposed to be can really work out for the best. So I recommend trying new things and don't let obstacles get in your way.

Chapter 19
Did I Really Need That Class?

I look at education differently than most people. Grades and degrees don't matter unless they are needed for your specific career. In over 4,500 production jobs I've worked on, I've never once been asked if I even have a degree. (I do)

When I was in college I went for a double major of art and business. I love being creative, but I wanted to also make money.

I took a number of marketing courses and loved them. At the same time, outside of school, I earned money by designing logos and print materials for local businesses.

I often cold-called local businesses to try and drum up new business. One day I walked into Nacogdoches Pool and Spa and spoke with the owner. I discovered that he was interested in investing in some billboards.

I always try to tell a story with every project. Since I was in college, I always had sex and girls on my mind and hot tubs just screamed sex. So I created a billboard concept whose image told a story that most buyers would understand. Buy this spa…and you'll get laid.

The owner loved the idea and hired me.

Once he approved my rough sketch, I produced a photo session. I hired the hottest girl at school and posed her in a bikini in a spa. (for some reason, the spa owner hung around for the photo shoot) Then I transformed the photo into an illustration since drawings, back then, were cheaper than photos for printing billboards.

Nacogdoches is a small town, only about 24,000 people including 12,000 college students. But the spa owner still put up two of my billboards.

The crazy thing was every time I drove from my house to school for my marketing courses, I drove past the two billboards I had designed.

Figure 44 - I passed this billboard, which I designed, on my way to school to study marketing.

I couldn't tell you any of the grades I got in college, but I do remember the big lessons that I learned. That's the true value of education.

The benefits of education also never end. To this day I still study and learn.

A few years ago when I lived in Orlando, I heard about a storyboarding course in New York taught by two artists from Pixar. I decided to attend it.

To give you a little backstory, I'm mostly known for my storyboarding work. I have worked on thousands of productions, wrote the bible of the industry, *Storyboards: Motion In Art*, and helped develop the main storyboarding software, Storyboard Pro.

I flew to NY excited to attend and meet the men teaching the course.

There was a long line outside the Gem Hotel in Soho where the course was held. The doors stayed closed until the class started, so many of us stood around and talked.

One of the guys in line looked over at me and did a double take. "Aren't you Mark Simon?" A few other people stopped talking and looked over at me.

"Yes I am."

He got a quizzical look on his face. "Dude. What are you doing here? You literally wrote the book on storyboarding! You should be teaching this class, not attending it."

At this point a bunch of people recognized me and moved forward. A couple of them even had my book with them and pulled them out.

Figure 45 - The line I stood in to get into the Pixar story session.

I looked around at everyone and replied, "I'm here because I always want to improve. I figured if I only learn one thing from Pixar, it will have been worth the cost and trip."

I saw a true look of shock on most of their faces.

I constantly try to improve.

If you want to stay relevant in whatever you do, you need to stay on top. Do you invest in your learning? Do you keep up with new techniques and new software? If not, your career may be limited and you won't give your clients everything they deserve.

There's no way to start at the top if your knowledge is out of date.

Section 4
Tell Other People
What to Do

If you have read various books on business or listen to business leaders talk about what makes a great boss, you will hear lots of conflicting ideas. That's because different things work for different people.

My best friend growing up often said, "I won't ask someone to do something I'm not willing to do."

Sounds admirable. But he and I differ there.

I don't want to scrub toilets. But I have no problem telling someone else to 'clean that shit up'.

I also don't ask people who work for me to do their job. I tell them. Asking gives people the option to say 'no'. If you work for me, I don't want you to have that option. If it's your job, do it.

However, if I would like someone to do something outside of the job they were hired for, I will ask them to do it.

Equal partnerships also seldom work. One person always needs to have final say in case of a stalemate. No decision is often worse than a bad decision.

I have high expectations for those around me. That includes my employees, the people I work for and my family and friends. You'd be surprised how often people rise to an occasion if you give the chance…or a gentle shove.

There have been times when I've expected people to do something outside of what is normally expected or assumed in any particular industry. I didn't feel I was out of line. I felt the rest of the industry norm was wrong, and I have no problem challenging norms I disagree with. The chapter on a confrontation I had with one of my publishers is a good example. As the author, I owned the product. I expect the publisher to support my wishes. They expected me to sit back and be quiet. One of us got a shock…and it wasn't me.

But I will ask you to read the following stories of my telling other people what to do and how to take control of a situation.

Chapter 20
Be Your Own Boss

Do you like to tell other people what to do? Do you like to be the boss of every project and everything that you're a part of? Are you also willing to take a risk? Well, then you very well might be an entrepreneur.

There's a lot more to entrepreneurship and running a business, than just being bossy and telling people what to do. You do have to understand all the different aspects of business. You have to understand accounting. You have to understand marketing. You have to understand salesmanship. You have to be willing to get after people you may consider friends. You have to be willing to eat crow to clients - not all the time - but when necessary. You have to be willing to do whatever it takes, and work whatever hours needed. Like all of them.

Being an entrepreneur is not an instant cash cow. It means that you will likely struggle for a while as you figure out how to make things work. Most entrepreneurs will tell you that they hit harder times before they hit better times, but a true entrepreneur only sees the benefits and the positive and goes for it, no matter what.

That doesn't mean you shouldn't pay attention to mistakes and problems. You do. You should be willing to take ideas from other people, not just when they offer it but pay attention to people both in your field and in other fields. If they're successful, why? What are they doing that makes them successful?

I remember going to a local Chamber of Commerce event and I noticed that the people working at the sign-in table ran some of the biggest companies around and I thought, "Why would the owners of these great companies be working at the sign-in table at this event?"

And then it hit me. They knew everybody there. And they didn't work the sign-in table because they knew everybody. They knew everybody because they worked the sign-in table.

The great thing about working the sign-in table, is you meet everybody as they come in and your job is over by the time the event starts and you can enjoy the rest of the event.

And as you walk around you've already met most of the attendees and you know exactly who they work with, what their company is, and it gives you the opportunity to speak with them and know them by name. You've already broken the ice at the sign-in table.

As much as you may hate accounting, learn it. Accounting is your money and you need to know where it is.

Everyone's a salesman. Every business is based on sales. If you can't sell, you can't make money.

You have to learn all the different aspects of your business.

One of the best pieces of advice that my father ever gave me when I went to college, he said, "Study anything you want as long as you also study business." I walked out of college with a double major of art and business because art is business. Entertainment is business. Everything is business.

As a serial entrepreneur - I've started a number of companies - I can tell you that you need to pay attention to all the different aspects of what it takes to run a business. Don't just think that you'll be successful because of your passion. You need the passion, but you need the business knowledge just as much.

Chapter 21
Author or Publisher – Who's the Boss?

Your success as a published author has a lot to do with attitude; your attitude, and the attitude of those you work with.

Over the years I've had a number of books published. I came up with one idea which I thought would be huge. My *Facial Expression* series of books.

Figure 46 – Facial Expressions is a series of books which are photo references for artists. I took 50 models, photographed them from all different angles as they held a variety of expressions. I started the first book as reference for myself and the artists who work for me.

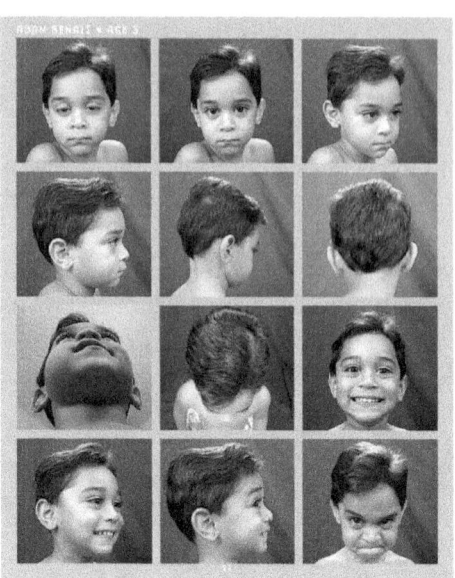

Figure 47 - A page from my Facial Expressions - Babies to Teens book.

As I put together the huge photo collection of faces, I realized, "Wow I'm not the only one who needs this."

I put together a book proposal and took it to my current publisher. They wanted it and offered me a contract. However, I held off signing the contract. I wanted a bigger publisher than the one I was currently signed to.

I researched publishers and Watson-Guptill was one of the biggest book publishers in art books. I found the contact information for the publisher, contacted her, and pitched her the idea. It caught her attention. She asked for a book proposal which I sent her. She then made an offer on my book.

I then had the two publishers actually bid against each other for the rights to my book. There were a few things I wanted in my deal. One, I wanted to keep the copyright. A lot of book publishers in their default contract have you sign over the copyright. I wasn't going to do that. Most authors simply don't know any better.

Both agreed to that demand. I also wanted to see who could get my books into more markets and book stores and

Watson-Guptill had more influence than my other publisher.

I also wanted marketing for my book, and Watson-Guptill offered a bigger marketing campaign. So I ended up going with Watson-Guptill. I signed the contract and delivered the book.

As we finished the book, we started to work on promotion. That included where I should speak, what marketing materials they planned to provide such as posters, banners, ads, and more.

I got on the phone one day as we prepared for one of my public speeches. There were three women on the phone with me - all from Watson-Guptill - my editor, someone from publicity, and the other was the production manager who oversaw my book. They were my main contacts to help take the book to the next phase.

I told one of the ladies I needed something and told another I needed something else done. I wanted them to create various posters and ads. I needed them done a certain way. I discussed the schedule we needed to hit, and what I needed from them to support my upcoming talk.

When I finished my description, there was silence on the phone. One of the women eventually said, "Mark, we don't work for you. We dictate all these elements."

My response was, "Actually, you do work for me and this is what we need to make this book successful."

They started argue and said, "No, we're the publishers. We don't work for you. No author ever dictates what we do."

I then taught them a lesson. "I really don't care what other authors do. Their lack of understanding on what they own is their problem, not mine. I own this book. I'm letting you publish it. I'm licensing you the rights to sell it. I own it, therefore you do work for me. This is part of our contractual deal. Now, this is what we're going to do."

And they got really pissed at me and said, "No one has ever talked to us this way before."

I replied, "Again, that's not relevant. I don't care how other people work with you. If an author doesn't understand his own rights you're there to help, that's their problem not mine. I know exactly what my position is. You wanted this book. We all know this is going to be successful and I want to work together but make no mistake - I own this property."

The rest of the call was tense, but they eventually did everything I asked them to do.

Many people need to understand where their power is and be willing to fight for it. You need to understand the realities of any situation because you are not always going to have the power. But you also have to realize it doesn't matter what other people have done in the past if it conflicts with what you need now. The past is only the past. It's something to learn from, it's not something to hold you back.

Chapter 22
Do Your Fucking Job

Working conditions are usually best when people are polite with each other. But there are times when a brutal response is needed to break a stagnation and get something done.

Years ago we were hired through an outside agency to draw comic-book style marketing illustrations of Indian action star Shahrukh Khan (aka: G.One) for his super hero movie *Ra-One*. He wanted a comic look to the marketing art and to have the illustrated face to look just like him.

Luckily one of the artists I work with is Alex Saviuk, who had drawn Spider-Man with Stan Lee for over 20 years, along with drawing Hulk, Superman, Phantom and others over the past 30 years. He had also drawn the *X-Files* comic book, which we used as proof of how accurately his drawings captured actors faces.

We finalized the contract which included 3 different illustrations and 3 revisions per illustration. Everyone was excited and Alex did and amazing job on the first pass.

Then we started to get notes.

Shahrukh didn't think the face looked like him. (It was a fantastic likeness) Alex did a revision and we got more notes back. Every set of notes pushed the likeness further and further from a good likeness, but the star was eventually happy with one face from one angle.

We discovered that he didn't see himself the way the world sees him. He is an Indian actor with a broad nose. Quite a handsome man. But somehow he saw himself with a very lean and narrow nose, which completely changes someone's looks.

ILLUSTRATION - 1

the face of this illustration needs to be replaced. the below illustration has the correct face. the style and the body language of the illustration has to be the same as Alex's.

correct illustration of the face

these is the final look poster image just for reference

Figure 48 - Notes we got from the client. Notice that the nose in the top image is MUCH closer to the photo than the narrow nose the client wanted to see. The face he liked was one we had done as one of the revisions, but the older images looked more like him.

As we finished our contracted amount of art and revisions, the star came back to us with more notes, he wanted his nose thinner again. However, we had exhausted both the number of contracted revisions and Alex's patience. Alex did not want to work on the project any longer. I didn't blame him.

I reached out to the agency to tell them that we needed a new contract for more revisions and that I would find a new artist to move forward. The actor even had the balls to go behind my back to Alex to try and get him to keep working on the art. (it didn't work)

The client was increasingly not happy with art he had previously approved. He said he refused to pay. We went back and forth and we got nowhere.

The agent came back to me and said he understood our position and the contract, but felt caught in the middle. He shrugged and said, "What do you want me to do?"

I was pissed at the run-around and yelled into the phone, "I want you to do your fucking job! We delivered. Get us paid. Nothing happens until they settle up!"

About the most the agent could say at that point was, "ummmm." He wasn't used to an artist speaking to him that way.

Agents work for artists. When I told him to do his fucking job, it got done. It pushed him to do what he should have already done. We got paid quickly.

I never like having to jump on someone, but I have no problem with it if I have to.

Chapter 23
Confidence is Everything

A confident attitude sells.

But you can have confidence and still be a dick. And being a dick is not a good attitude.

If you ask a girl out and you approach her with, "Oh, hi, I don't know, maybe you might, maybe, kind of-- you might not want to, but, you know, maybe do something, some kind of-- well, you probably don't," she will probably say 'No' because you have no confidence and a weak and lousy attitude.

But if you approach a woman with confidence, "Hey, Jeanne, you doing anything later? Want to go have dinner? Come on, I've got a great place. I'd love to take you to this amazing restaurant I know. You interested?" The chances of her saying yes, is extremely high. So you want to exude confidence in most situations.

There is one thing to keep in mind. In business, you really should know what you're talking about. Back up your confidence with knowledge. When you want to lead a situation, you should know as much as possible about what's going on. Take that extra time, read up, study up, and be prepared.

An inquisitive attitude is also something that people love to be around. When you work with a lot of people and you ask their opinion, you ask for their knowledge. You're telling them that they know something you don't and you value their knowledge. That's powerful. Especially when you then take that information and you use it, make use of it, and give that person credit when credit is due.

A lot of people are afraid to speak in public. Do you know when people aren't afraid to give a public talk? When they are confident and they know what they're talking about.

When you are confident about a subject matter, you don't worry about what word to say first, or what the third sentence should be.

I do a lot of public speaking and I never memorize my talks. I don't have to. I will not give a talk unless I am absolutely confident about what I plan to talk about. When I'm confident the talk becomes easy and fun.

When you are confident and have fun, people will be drawn to you.

A few years ago I gave a talk at San Diego Comic-Con. Comic-Con, if you're not familiar with it, is the largest event about comics, pop culture and media in the United States. It's 145,000 people who descend on San Diego every July.

I was speaking about storyboarding, which is the visual comic book-like blueprint of a movie or animation script. I own a storyboarding company and I wrote the main industry book that everyone learns from, Storyboards: Motion In Art, 3rd Edition. I've been to Comic-Con a number of times but to be able to speak there is a huge opportunity.

Figure 49 - My talk at Comic-Con.
I had no screen to show my work,
but my attitude sold the crowd on my abilities.

I started my talk to a standing room only crowd. The room was supposed to hold about 350 seated people but there were also people lining the walls. The energy in the room was great.

I gave it everything I had, but I wasn't able to show any samples. It was just me on the stage talking about the visual art form of storyboarding. I spoke about how I liked to work with directors, and about production stories and how I got started in the industry. I held that audience in the palm of my hand as I confidently regaled them with my production stories.

At one point I asked the crowd, "If you had a production starting and you needed storyboards, how many of you would hire me to do your storyboarding?"

Almost everybody in the room raised their hand. I looked at them, smiled and said, "Why would you hire me? None of you have seen any of my work. I haven't shown you any of my work."

They laughed (thankfully).

Every person in that room was ready to hire me without seeing my samples. Why? Because of my confidence. I spoke with passion and confidence about storyboarding. I spoke with an absolute certainty of the best way to storyboard and how I helped productions.

I was confident so they were confident in me. If you inspire confidence, you will get hired.

Section 5
Prove It, Don't Just Say It

Do you remember those people in your life who were blowhards? The ones who would say how great they would be at something, but never actually did anything?

I remember them. They annoyed the shit out of me. Don't tell me how easy something is if you've never tried it.

I don't want to be that person who talks a big story without backing it up. So I do things.

When I wanted to work in animation, I created a portfolio of animation samples to prove what I could do.

When I saw people struggling to do something I had experience with, I opened my mouth and offered suggestions based on actual experience and real knowledge.

When I saw a new technology I wanted to learn, I talked my way into free access to that tech and became an invaluable resource.

When I wanted to move into a new career, I found someone to give me notes and suggestions. When they told me how bad my samples were but offered to review new samples, I kept going back until I was good enough that I got hired.

Actions speak louder than words. But, since this book can only hold words, I'll tell about my actions.

Chapter 24
Get a Promotion In Hours, Not Years

You've probably heard the expression that actions speak louder than words, and nothing could be more true than when you're trying to attain success.

I'm a big believer in proving to people what you can do by doing it. You can talk until you're blue in the face, but words really don't mean anything without action supporting them.

Years ago, after I graduated college, I moved out to Los Angeles. I wanted to work in Hollywood.

Hollywood was a dream. When I moved out there, I didn't know anybody. I didn't have any film or TV experience, besides some stuff in college. Nothing professional. In very little time I started working in Hollywood. I started working at a set design company and then started landing freelance jobs. On my first movie - called *Slave Girls from Beyond Infinity* - I had become art director within 2 weeks.

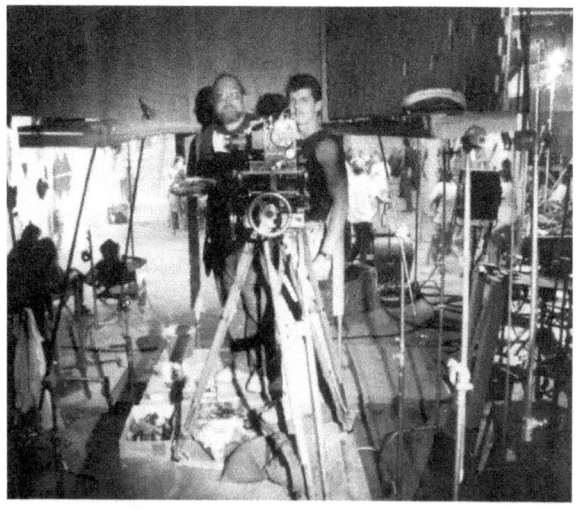

Figure 50 - Working on the foreground miniatures on the set of Slave Girls Beyond Infinity at Roger Corman's studio.
I'm the one without sleeves.

Someone who had worked for me on that movie had landed a high-end commercial job and called me up late at night to ask if I would be a P.A., production assistant, for her the next morning.

"No," I said. "I'm not interested in that. I don't P.A. I'm an art director."

She replied, "Oh, come on, please, please. I really need your help. I'm kind of stuck. We start shooting first thing tomorrow, and one of the assistants I had booked bailed on me. Look at it this way. You'll make a couple extra bucks and you'll meet some people. It's for N. Lee Lacy & Associates, a big production company. Please, I need some help. As a favor for me?"

I said, "All right. As a favor for you, I'll do it."

Call time was the next morning at 6:30. I was a P.A., and the first thing they ask me to do was something I truly did not know how to do; make coffee. I know it sounds weird, but I didn't know how to make coffee. I actually still don't know how to make coffee. I don't like the smell of coffee so I avoid it completely. I've never had a cup.

On my first job as a P.A., I had to literally say "No" to the very first thing they asked me to do. That's usually a bad way to start a job.

I told the producer, "Look, I'll do anything else you guys need, but I have no idea how to make coffee, so no one would be happy with it."

The producer rolled her eyes and gave me other things to do around the set. I wasn't sure I would last the day.

The commercial was for a bank. We were in a closed location that looked like a bank, and there was a couple of hours of setup before we could start shooting. I ran around doing whatever little menial things they'd ask me to do, but I did each one to the best of my abilities.

I noticed that there was a group of ladies working on some sort of sign on the floor. They were trying to put it together as one of the set decorations.

Figure 51 - The commercial shoot where I moved from production assistant to running the art department by noon.

As I walked by the women, I glanced over and saw what they were trying to do. I had put together signs like that during my advertising days and knew exactly how to help them. I stopped really quickly and pointed out what they needed to do and I walked on.

I walked by a few minutes later and saw they were struggling with something else. I offered my help again and I rushed off to finish my next chore.

I walked by a few times and I kept making little comments, just trying to be helpful. Eventually, one of the ladies looked up and stopped me. She said, "Hold on a minute. What are you doing here?"

"I'm a P.A. I'm helping out a friend." I replied.

She said, "Why do you know so much about what we're doing?"

"Oh, I'm actually an art director. I'm just here as a favor for the day. I've got a large background in construction and design. I've spent most of my life designing and putting things together."

She smiled and looked at the others she was working with. "OK, you're no longer a P.A."

I thought, "Uh, oh. She heard about the coffee incident."

She continued, "You're working with us now. I want you running this art department." And that was it. In less than two hours, I went from being a PA to running the art department on the series of commercials.

N. Lee Lacy & Associates and owner and director, N. Lee Lacy, was one of the biggest commercial companies and directors in Hollywood in the mid-'80s. They turned into a long-time and profitable client of mine. I designed a tremendous number of commercials for them, all because I accepted a new opportunity.

I could have just minded my own business and done my job as a P.A. But by helping other people, showing what I knew, and been willing to talk about my background, and my abilities, it gave them the opportunity to give me a better job.

You can be the best in the world at what you do, but if no one knows it, they don't have the opportunity to hire you and to pay you for your expertise. Be willing, at all times, to prove what you can do.

Chapter 25
Late Night Study Leads to NBC

In order to jump into a new career field, you need to prove you can do something, not just say you can do it. The concept behind prove it, don't say it is: in order to get someone to believe you can do something, telling them you can do it isn't enough. It's not proof. But if you want to advance in a job, get a promotion to move to something new, you need to have proof you can do it.

Prove you can do it by doing it.

I once landed a network gig by proving I could do a job, before I even knew a job was available.

When CG (computer generated) animation and illustration first started becoming possible in the early 90's, there were programs that most people had never even heard about. Most people didn't have computers that could handle the requirements of the high-end software. I didn't own a computer that was fast enough for doing CG animation much less any high-end graphic software because the software suites alone were anywhere from $5,000, $10,000, to $15,000 a piece. But creating images and animation in a computer sounded really cool and I wanted to play with the new graphic softwares.

When I worked at Nickelodeon on the Universal Orlando lot, an owner of a production company on the lot, in Building 22, the main production office building on the lot, was investing in new technology. I heard that he had purchased an incredible computer and graphics program that could do network quality computer painting. It was a program called Rio, which was a precursor to programs like Photoshop. He also had a 3D animation program installed on the system. It all sounded really freaking cool.

I walked over to his office one night after work and introduced myself to him.

I went to his office and just knocked on his door. I had met him briefly at an industry event earlier in the year, so I figured he would at least recognize me.

He invited me in. I spoke to him about my work at Nickelodeon, things I wanted to do and how I heard he had painting and 3D computer programs. I asked, "Would you mind showing them to me?"

He replied enthusiastically, "Oh, I'd love to." He was so proud. People love to talk about themselves and to show off things they've invested in.

He led me into the office next to his. It was a big open room filled with desks and a few new computers. The room looked like no one worked in it.

He sat down and he started to show me what his computers and software could do by running some demos that came with the software.

I said, "This looks incredible. Do you ever have any downtime on this system when no one is using it? I'd love to spend some time here and teach myself? I can come in late at night or whenever works for you."

"Actually, I do." He said with a grin, "Not many people know how to use any of this software, I'd be happy to let you Learn."

Having access like that to computers I couldn't afford was incredible. Every night I would go in, spend hours reading through the books, go through demos and aught myself how to do CG animation and how to use the Rio paint program.

I don't remember how long that went on – Maybe four or five weeks. The owner eventually gave me a key to his office. He came in every so often to check on me and see samples of my test creations.

One night when he came in and was all excited, "Hey, I want to share something with you."

He told me he had landed a deal for a TV show called *Firefighters*. It was a show for NBC and it was kind of like the show *Cops* where camera crews follow actual cops during drive-arounds, busting people, chase them down, and that kind of thing. His concept was to do the same thing with real Firefighters.

One of the segments of his show featured the ATF, which is the Alcohol, Tobacco and Firearms, a division of the U.S. government.

He told me, "You have probably seen their Most Wanted posters. We want to digitally clean up their 'wanted' photos have some graphics of each wanted poster created digitally and we are starting production immediately. No one else knows how to use our system. Would you like to do the graphics and 3D for us?"

The next thing I knew, I was creating graphics for an NBC series.

Talking about creating computer graphics would not have gotten me the job. Creating samples did. Showing up every day without pay and teaching myself how to use the software gave the producer confidence in me. That confidence turned into a paycheck and a great credit.

Chapter 26
Going Back, Again and Again

My second career in Hollywood has been as a storyboard artist. I enjoyed art directing, my first Hollywood career, but I found that I really missed drawing.

As an art director on movies, storyboards came across my desk quite often. I thought it looked like a lot of fun, a lot like drawing comic books. Storyboards illustrate a director's vision of the script, much like blueprints show a crew how the architect wants to house built.

To change my career to storyboarding, I did what I usually do. I started at the top. I introduced myself to the biggest and best storyboard agency in the biz. At that point it was a company called Storyboards, Inc., based in Venice, an area of Los Angeles.

I drove to their offices and walked in. I asked if there was an agent that I could speak with. John, one of the agents asked me to join him at his desk.

I explained that I was an art director and wanted to transition to storyboarding. John asked for samples and I pulled out what I'd created on my own. I was very excited to show how great my samples were.

My samples were terrible. They were laid out wrong. Formatting was wrong. He pointed out that basically that my work had everything wrong you could possibly have.

I just didn't know any better. I drew samples based on no experience. The agent very patiently explained to me what was wrong with my work. Then he gave me some little half page promotional flyers of some of their more popular story artists.

As John escorted me to the door, he said, "These are examples of what our clients expect to see. This is what we would need to see from you."

I nodded and said, "Okay. I can do that."

As I approached the door he said, "Look, any time you want, you can come back in and I'm happy to look at your new stuff."

I thanked him and left with the samples he had pulled for me.

I was working at HBO at that time so every night I would draw up new storyboard samples.

A week later I showed back up at Storyboards, Inc.

John was good to his word and he sat with me to review my new work. "Okay, let's take a look. Oh yeah, these are a lot better. Look, here's a couple more things you can do," and he gave me some more tips on how to improve my work. John told me to concentrate on a short action sequence with a beginning, middle and end.

I replied, "Okay." I went away, and a week later I showed up again.

John looked up from his desk and was shocked to see me standing there again, "Oh. Most people don't come back. This is great. Okay." He reached out for the new samples he knew I had brought. My samples were full of short action bits as he suggested. John nodded a bit as he reviewed my new work and gave me a few more tips.

His comment about most people not returning really hit me. I was evidently unusual simply because I came back.

I went away and I came back again the following week. In fact, I would go back every week to see John with new and improved samples.

Finally on one of my visits, he looked at my work and then at me, smiled and said, "You want a commercial?"

"Hell yeah!" I replied excitedly. "I'd love one."

"Okay. You're ready." He gave me a Volkswagen commercial right then and there. We hadn't signed any paperwork, but he told me what their commission would be and told me that they needed someone right away.

That afternoon I started storyboarding on a Volkswagen commercial. My first professional storyboard gig. That quickly lead to storyboarding an episode on *1st & 10*, an HBO football satire series.

The lesson I learned from that experience with the agency was, by showing up again and again and advancing, improving, it will often lead to a job.

I currently own a storyboard studio. I review storyboard artist samples quite often. When I have time, I try to give notes like John had given me. Of all the artists who I've given notes, only a few have ever come back to show me new and revised samples.

I've hired many of those few artists who have returned with updated work.

99.9% of the people whose stuff I review, I never hear from again. Even if I liked their work, I'm not always in a position to hire someone at any single moment. By following up, artists are more likely to reach me at a time when I need someone.

I'm not going to hire someone who's not willing to put in the effort to improve. But if you do, and you keep coming back, that tells me a few things. One, you really want to do it. Two, it means that you're going to be a good worker because you can take notes. Three, it means you'll probably finish a job because you're willing to do what it takes to deliver.

Chapter 27
I Got Wizard of Id

Actions speak louder than words.

Years ago my wife, Jeanne, and I had dinner with a college friend of hers, Lisa Godsick, and Lisa's husband, Chris Godsick. Lisa and Chris had met as agents working at the William Morris Agency.

During dinner Chris told us the story of how one of his WMA clients had been the amazing Chinese film director, John Woo. He is the director of such films as *Face/Off*, *Paycheck, Mission: Impossible II, Broken Arrow* and others.

John had left Los Angeles to begin working on a new movie overseas. Chris made the decision that he wanted to produce rather than act as an agent. And he wanted to produce for John Woo.

But, he didn't want to tell John his wishes over the phone. He thought that wouldn't make a big enough impression and he only had one shot to land a partnership that big.

So Chris bought himself an airline ticket to fly halfway around the world to where John Woo was prepping his next film.

John was shocked when Chris showed up at his door and was suitably impressed when Chris told him why he had chased him around the world. Chris became John Woo's producing partner on movies like *Broken Arrow* and *Face/Off*.

At dinner, I told Chris I would remember that story for when I needed to make that type of impression.

Many years later, I had the opportunity to make use of Chris's inspiration.

I am a huge fan of comic strips. I grew up reading every comic strip in the newspaper and cartoonists were my heroes. My favorites were *Peanuts* (of course), *Dennis the Menace, B.C.* (the cartoon cavemen), *Wizard of Id, Bloom County, Marmaduke, Doonesbury* and others. I read everything

I could find about every artist. I bought every cartoon book I could.

Figure 52 - One of many bookshelves I have filled with cartoon books.

In 2007, I had been teaching storyboarding at the DAVE School (Digital Animation & Visual Effects) in between production gigs. The school was founded by Jeff and Anne Scheetz, who had become good friends of mine.

Jeff and I were talking on the phone one day and he asked me if I remembered one of our students from a few years earlier, Mason Mastroianni.

"Sure," I replied. I remembered Mason as being very talented. He designed some of the space ships for a project I had written for Jeff called *NASA Seals*.

"His grandfather, Johnny Hart, just passed away," Jeff told me. "Mason just went home to take over his comic strip, *B.C.*"

I felt like I had just been slapped.

"Mason was Johnny Hart's grandson!?" I blurted out in disbelief.

"Yeah. You didn't know?"

"Shit no, I didn't know!" My head was reeling. I had been that close to the family of one of my heroes. Not only did Johnny Hart create *B.C.*, but he also created *Wizard of Id*, which was drawn by Brant Parker. I LOVED those strips growing up and still read them online.

Figure 53 - Holding a couple of my favorite comic strip books.

Jeff laughed. "Sorry, Man. I thought you knew. Mason didn't really talk about it much."

I barely heard Jeff, because I instantly had ideas of what could be done with both comic strips. They deserved to be made into movies and TV series. I needed to get ahold of Mason.

"Do you have a phone number for Mason?" I asked.

"No. I just have his email. I can give that to you," replied Jeff.

Jeff sent me Mason's email. I made plans on what I would do next with this new information. I wanted to meet with Mason and his family and pitch them the idea of my creating and pitching TV shows and movies based on their characters.

In the 30 years I've been working in the entertainment industry, I've created, sold and landed over 35 production and distribution deals. I know how to pitch ideas to studios.

But I didn't want to pitch Mason over the phone or by email. I wanted to do it in person. I knew I had to invest in my pitch to Mason and his family. I needed to travel and see them in person, just like Chris did to pitch himself to John Woo.

I sent Mason a few emails to express my condolences about the loss of his grandfather. I also mentioned that I wanted to speak with him about the strips.

But I didn't get any response. None. We had gotten along well when he was in my class, but we hadn't gotten close. I didn't know if he was ignoring my emails or not receiving them or putting them aside. But, I wasn't going to let that stop me. I was on a quest to work with his properties.

I searched the web for phone numbers. I found information about the John Hart Studios, but didn't find any phone numbers on any websites.

I kept searching for a number so I could speak to someone. On one of my Google searches, many, many pages down, showed the name John Hart Studios and it had a phone number in the search listing. I clicked on the link, but the linked page was dead. I went back to the search listings and copied down the phone number.

When I called the number an elderly lady answered the phone. I introduced myself, gave my condolences, mentioned what a huge fan I was, said that I was one of Mason's teachers and was hoping to talk to them about their comic strips. I didn't know who the person was but she said that she would have to have someone else get back to me.

The good news is that conversation told me that I had found a still-working phone number. The bad news is I never heard back from anybody.

I called back again a day or two later and left a voice message and got no response.

I really wanted to speak to them so I called again the following week. That time a younger woman answered the phone, who I soon found out was Patti Hart, Johnny Hart's eldest daughter, and Mason's mother. Instead of introducing myself, I started with, "I am not looking for money. I will bring you the money." Then I introduced myself. She didn't hang up on me.

I had figured that one of the reasons they ignored me earlier was they probably thought I wanted them to fund a production. I'm sure a lot of people call them expecting them to be ultra-wealthy and wanting them to fund something. So I got that out-of-the-way immediately and I got her attention.

She explained that it was her mother, the widow of Johnny Hart, who answered the phone the previous week. She then confirmed that they didn't return my call because they thought I was looking for money.

I explained a bit about my background, how I knew Mason, that I was a gigantic fan of the strips and that I would love to fly to their studio and give them a proposal. I told him I would get myself there in the next week. I asked her directly what day worked for them. We planned on the following Friday. I was flying high.

We set up a time, she told me where their studio was and recommended the best place for me to stay. We hung up and then the real work began.

I had just over a week to put together a killer proposal that would inspire them to give me the rights to their comic strips so I could develop them up as movies and TV series and allow me to pitch their strips to the networks and studios.

My first phone call was to my agent. I told him to prepare an option agreement that I could take on my trip.

He only sounded slightly interested. He's heard lots of promises and big ideas from me and other clients.

The next thing on my list was finding my magic bullet. I wanted something so spectacular for my presentation that they would have to say "Yes."

I called Heather Kenyon, an old friend of mine from when I wrote for her when she was the editor-in-chief at *Animation World Network*, http://www.awn.com.

Heather had since become vice president of development at Starz Animation up in Toronto. I've always liked her and we stayed in touch over the years. When I got Heather on the phone, I told her I had an upcoming meeting and a connection with the owners of the comic strips in *B.C.* and *Wizard of Id*.

She told me she was a big fan of both strips and asked what she could do to help. I told her that I was going to fly up to the studio and try to close the deal for the rights. I asked her if she would call me at noon on the pitch day and if she would be willing to tell them that if they signed a deal with me she would want to work with us to create movies based on their properties.

She agreed. It was all coming together! But I still had a lot of work to do to get ready for my presentation.

I needed to create pitch packages to support my concepts and to give them more information on what I've done and how many shows I have sold.

I booked my flight, rented a car and flew to upstate New York and drove out to their studio.

Figure 54 - Driving to the John Hart Studio in upstate NY.

We planned to have dinner the night before my pitch so we could get to know each other. We got along instantly.

I met with Patti and her two sons, Mason and his younger brother Mick. Mick was one of the writers of the comic strips and Mason was writing and drawing *B.C.*

As we walked into their favorite Italian restaurant and towards our table, the boys were bitching back-and-forth with their mother good-heartedly like a lot of families do. As we approach the table Patti threw her hands up in the air and said loudly and unapologetically for all to hear, "Bitch, bitch, bitch!" We sat down and I laughed. She was my new best friend.

We had a great time and a lot of laughs at dinner. It was a fantastic way to build a relationship without talking any business at all.

I showed up at their studio the next morning right on time. They gave me a tour, which was one of the greatest treats of my life. All the artwork and all the art supplies used to create two of my favorite comic strips were right there in front of me. I was eight years old again.

I watched my time to make sure I started my presentation with enough time to be ready for Heather's surprise phone call.

Figure 55 - The table at John Hart Studios where I pitched myself. Mason is seated and his brother Mick stands to the side.

My pitch went great. I had a ton of energy, which is easy when you love the subject. About halfway through my pitch, Ida Hart, Johnny's widow, entered. She was all smiles and I adored her instantly.

As it approached noon I told them that I knew the studios I could get the pitch to so the right eyes would see it and I was the best person to take it to market.

No sooner had I finished my pitch than my phone rang.

I smiled and said, "Let me take this. I think it's for all of us."

I answered and put it on speakerphone. I said, "Heather, this is Mark. I've got you on speakerphone with the family behind *B.C.* and *Wizard of Id.*"

Heather was great. I introduced her, where she worked and Heather filled in the rest. She told them what a big fan she was of their properties and that she knew why I was there. She said if they signed a deal with me, she would like to bring the properties into Starz to turn them into movies.

We talked for just a couple minutes and I let Heather go.

The Hart family was thrilled. They kept talking between each other how exciting it was to talk to the head of a studio so quickly. I had proved I had the connections to fulfill my promises.

Patti held her hand out and asked if I had a contract with me. I said I did, pulled it out and handed it to her. She read through it, spoke to the family for a minute and grabbed a pen. She started to sign the Option Agreement.

My heart was beating a million miles a minute. I couldn't believe what was happening. As they were signing, I stepped aside and called my agent. I got him on the phone and said, "Matt, they're signing it."

He questioned me, "Signing what?"

"They're signing the option agreement right now!"

He said the contract was only a rough draft. "I didn't think you would get them to actually sign it today."

I told him, "Well, I hope you know what you're doing because that's the one they're signing."

He was shocked, but thrilled, and I hung up.

The hard part was over. I knew what their objections were likely to be. I approached everything with, "I am bringing all of this to you and I'm the one with the connections to make it happen." It worked.

I done what I had flown up there to do. Using Chris's experience as inspiration truly worked. I was fully prepared and I impressed them with investing in travel to their studio and everything I prepared for the pitch.

The best way to close any deal is to show the benefits to the client. What you, or your product, can do for them. When you go out of your way and invest in presenting to a potential client, they will be impressed.

Figure 56 - Celebrating signing our deal at John Hart Studios.
From the left, Mark Simon, Mick Mastroianni, Patti Hart,
and Mason Mastroianni.

Chapter 28
Tinker Bell

I love animation. Who doesn't love animation? It's the most creative thing you could possibly do. So of course I wanted to be an animator.

When I first moved to Los Angeles, I tried to become an animator but I never worked in an animation studio. I didn't know how to move my way up in the industry and what is expected. You don't start as an animator, you learn as you work your way up the animation ladder. But, as you've read in this book, I don't work that way.

In my initial quest to work in animation I was lucky enough to meet Bill Hanna and Joe Barbera. I went straight to the top, to the namesakes of Hanna-Barbera, creators of *The Flintstones*, *The Jetsons* and others. I told them I wanted to be an animator, showed them my stuff and they very quickly shot me down. They said I wasn't ready to be an animator.

Other design jobs soon came my way in live action production, so those jobs set the direction of my career for a number of years.

Years later, I was living in Orlando, and the animation process of digital ink and paint was just appearing. Prior to digital ink and paint we used to draw on paper, clean up the drawings on another piece of paper, and re-ink the drawings onto sheets of acetate, called a cel. Once the ink dries on the front of the cel, you flip it over and you paint one color at a time on the back of the acetates.

The entire process was very time consuming and very space consuming. But when digital ink and paint arrived it became much easier to produce animation in small area. We could draw on paper and scan it. The scanning would capture the pencil drawing instead of inking it, and then we could just drop-fill the colors into it. It was fun, it was quick, it took little space and it looked awesome.

I wanted to animate again. So I bought a digital ink and

paint software package and I started animating things for myself. I built a sample portfolio. Eventually I felt I was ready to produce for other people.

I always read through the trades, industry magazines, to keep up with the latest trends and happenings. Any industry you work in has their own trade magazines. You need to know what's going on, you need to know who is doing what, what's happening in the industry and who is who.

I read in one of the trades that a computer animation house, Lightpoint Entertainment, was moving onto the Disney Studio property in Orlando. The CEO of the company was Mark Kyle. I thought, "They're a CG house. I'll bet Disney or other companies are going to ask them to do work that's going to need 2-D animation and I'll bet they don't have 2-D animators on staff." I wanted to provide that service for them.

I called a friend of mine, Travis, who worked in Disney Feature Animation which was also on Disney Studio property. "Travis, it's Mark. Hey man, I need to get onto the backlot at Disney."

He asked, "Why?"

I laughed, "Does it matter?"

"Not really."

"Great, because I just need to get in. I need to find somebody on the backlot."

Travis was good to his word and got me a pass as if I was going to meet with him.

I drove into the studio the next day. I was on the giant Disney backlot, back behind scenes where all the offices and bungalows were. The only problem was I had no idea where the Lightpoint offices were. I walked around all the bungalows and office buildings but I didn't see any signs for it.

I walked into every bungalow and asked about Lightpoint. No one had heard of it. It was incredibly frustrating.

There I was with limited access to the Disney backlot

and I couldn't find the company I was looking for.

The only building I hadn't checked was a post-production house on the backlot. I didn't think one business would be located inside another, but I was out of options. I walked in and there was a door that separated the lobby from the rest of the place. There was a woman working behind the glass partition.

I asked her, "Is there any chance that Lightpoint is officed here?"

She replied, "Why, yes they are. They just moved in."

My eyes shot open in surprise. "Oh, thank God, that's awesome. Is the owner Mark available?"

She said, "He might be. It's just about lunch time. Let me check."

She came back and said, "He'll be right with you."

The door leading to the back creaked open a few inches, and Mark's face appeared. "Yes, can I help you?"

I reached out my hand to shake his and said, "Hi, my name is Mark Simon, and I'm a 2D animator."

He replied, "Yeah, but we do 3D."

I smiled and said, "I know, I know. And I'm not looking for a job. But I figure at some point someone's going to ask you to produce 2D animation, and I just want to be your source so you can say yes. I want you to be able to say yes to the gig, but you won't have to carry the overhead. I'll be that for you."

I pitched all benefits I could provide for him. Not what I wanted, but answers for what he may want.

He looked at me for a moment and I continued, "If you got a sec, I'd love to show you my stuff."

He thought for a moment, looked up and said, "I was just about to leave for lunch but, you know what? Yeah, I got a couple of minutes. Come on back."

He swung the door open and we walked back to his office. We sat down and I showed him samples of my animation. All the samples I'd created just for myself. None of the samples were for professional jobs, but I didn't tell him that. Telling someone samples were created for free or for a school project lessens their value. I let my work stand on its own.

He liked my animation samples and we hit it off and shared production stories. He looked from the TV monitor to me, smiled and asked if I wanted to see their latest project.

Mark started to show me an amazing piece that they were creating for the Disney Cruise Line. At that point the Disney Cruise Line hadn't opened yet. He showed me a computer animated version of the Disney Magic, the first boat Disney was building.

Mark pointed at the screen and said, "Disney wants Tinker Bell to fly up and touch the bow of the ship with her magic wand and transform a normal version of this ship into the Disney Magic ship."

I smiled at the implication, "That's a cool idea."

He continued, "But I don't think C.G. (computer generated) is the right way to go. I'd like it to look like the classic Tinker Bell from *Peter Pan*. Can you do that?"

Without hesitating I said, "Sure."

To this day I can't animate Tinker Bell to Disney quality. But I knew enough about animation and I knew there were other people I could hire who were better than me.

I walked out of that meeting with a $60,000 contract. My first professional animation was producing Tinker Bell for Disney. You can't get a better opening credit than Disney animation. That launched my first animation studio.

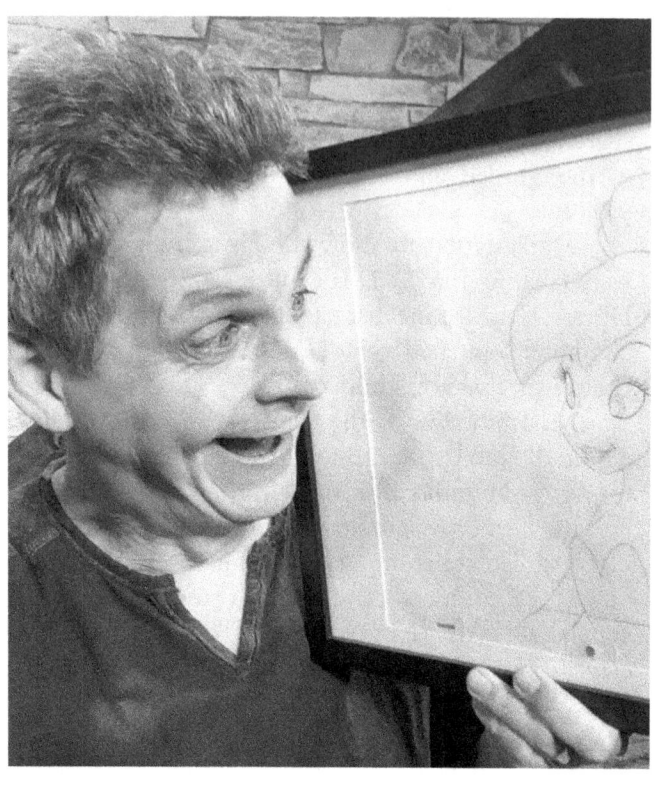

Figure 57 - Holding one of my original animation cells of Tinker Bell for the Disney Cruise Line.

If I had met with anyone but the owner of the studio, I wouldn't have had that opportunity. If I had wavered on whether or not I could do the job, I wouldn't have gotten the gig. If I had said my samples were not professional jobs I probably wouldn't have been offered the gig. If I hadn't read the industry trades, I wouldn't have known about Lightpoint at all. If I hadn't asked Travis for help, I couldn't have been in the right place at the right time.

That's a lot of ifs. Don't let an 'if' pass you by.

Section 6 - Fuck Ups

Starting at the top doesn't always work out. I have crashed and burned a few times.

Luckily, my average of succeeding is higher than the average of my disastrous fuck ups.

I look at failures in two ways:

1: I hope it makes a great story.

2: What can I learn from it?

I can't say I've always learned from my mistakes, but I try. More than anything I try not to repeat mistakes.

You may have heard the saying from Albert Einstein, "Insanity is doing the same thing over and over and expecting a different result." Some people may say I'm crazy, but at least I don't repeat my mistakes.

However, on the following page I will repeat some of the stories of my massive flame outs. Even if I didn't learn from them, I hope you do.

Chapter 29
Ego Got In The Way

There have been times in my life when my ego has gotten in the way of learning something and improving.

When I was attending Stephen F. Austin State University, SFA, my painting professor and I didn't completely see eye to eye. He was a good teacher, but I didn't listen or learn enough from him.

When I looked around the class, I was definitely one of the better artists at the beginning of the semester. That went to my head. I was cocky. I did my thing and only my thing. My paintings were good, but I didn't push myself or try to implement my professor's suggestions.

He pulled me aside one day. He asked for a ride back to his house. His car was broken down. As we walked out to the car and he said, "You know, you're probably the best artist I have in my painting class. But you're probably going to learn the least and grow the least."

I was shocked, "What do you mean?"

"Well, because you think you know more than you do, and you're less willing to listen and learn." His comments pissed me off.

I drove him to his house in a silent car. He stepped out and I drove away with his works echoing in my head. I was mad, but I didn't change.

Years later, I remember looking at some of my paintings and I finally understood and accepted what he had told me.

Do you remember when your parents would tell you a story or try to teach you a lesson and it didn't sink in until years later? Maybe you've tried to tell your kids something and they never got it.

That's what happened to me with his class. And I finalized realized that he was right. I recognized the same pattern of not listening in a number of other times in my life as well.

For instance, in electronics class. Because I built homes with my father growing up, I knew a lot about working with electricity. But, when I was in a class trying to teach me all the things I didn't know, I only half listened because I thought I knew more than I did.

Hopefully as an adult I'll remember that lesson and try to learn more. But it's amazing, looking back, how many opportunities in my life that would have made me better but my ego and false assumption of how much I knew got in my own way. It's a lesson now I hope I don't forget.

Chapter 30
Hanna-Barbera – Not This Time

Right after I moved out to Los Angeles, I wanted to work in animation. I was making the rounds and going to the different studios. Somehow - I don't remember how - I was able to get into Hanna-Barbera for a meeting with Bill Hanna and Joe Barbera, the founders of Hanna-Barbera. They are the creators of my childhood cartoons. The Flintstones. The Jetsons. Hong Kong Phooey. So many more. They are the biggest creators of animation in the 70's and 80's.

I look back at now and think, "Oh my god. I cannot believe I met with these two amazing men."

They shared an office in the Hanna-Barbera building, just across the 101 freeway from Universal Studios. I walked into their office and showed them my portfolio and some of the animation I had created in college.

Now, before I continue with this story, I'm going to give you a little history of my knowledge of animation. I'm completely self-taught. My university had an animation stand, but no one there understood animation. I had read some books on it, including the old Disney books like *The Illusion of Life*. This was the mid-80's, so there was no YouTube to learn from. I had full access to the animation stand and camera gear at school, but I was self-taught. But what I didn't know was…well, was a lot. I lacked knowledge that only a mentor, or working in the industry, or having a really good teacher could teach you.

That said, I found myself standing in the office of Bill Hanna and Joe Barbera showing them my portfolio. I was so proud…for a moment. Then they start ripping my work apart.

I went in wanting a job as an animator. I didn't know that you're supposed to work your way up, that you start as a clean-up artist and then move your way up to inbetween and then move your way up to animator. You learn how to be an animator by building your skills in the other animation roles. I didn't know that. I thought, "I'm just going to start as an animator." That's what my ego said.

When they start telling me, "You're not ready. You need a lot more experience. Maybe in five years, you'll be ready for something like this."

I thought, "Five years? I'm ready to start in five days."

Rather than learn and listen, I thank them for their time. As I was leaving - and I cannot believe I said this – but I did. "You'll be hearing of me before you hear from me."

That is probably the biggest dickish thing I have ever said, and I said it to two of my heroes.

I walked out. I can guarantee you, they never heard of me.

While I have a great story about meeting my heroes, I was a jerk to them - not one of my prouder moments.

Chapter 31
Self-Taught Failed Me This Time

As I mentioned in the previous chapter, I'm self-taught in animation. One of the problems with being self-taught is that there are industry standards you may not learn correctly, or at all.

For instance, animators use a dope sheet, also known as an X-Sheet, to organize all their drawings. The dope sheet is a frame-by-frame breakdown of all the layers and drawings and audio in a sequence. It's a blueprint of how to shoot and composite all the art in the correct order.

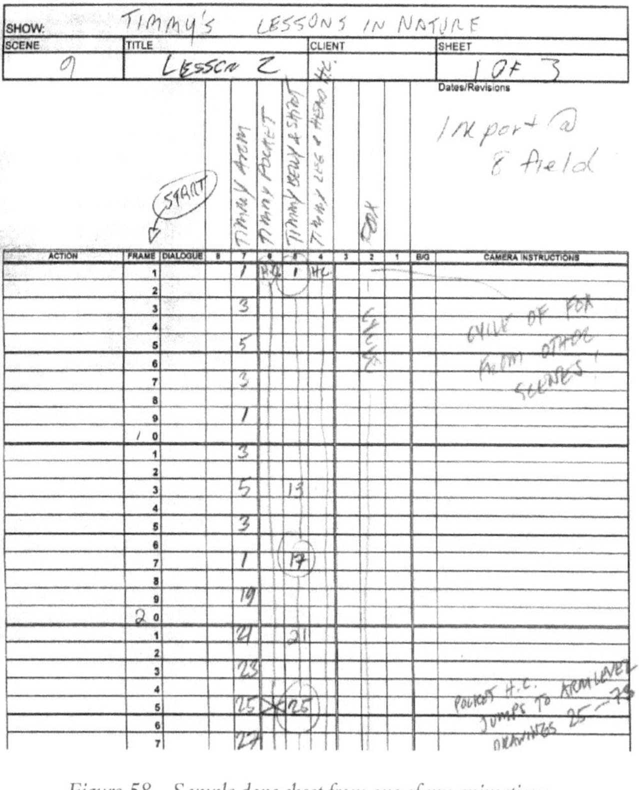

Figure 58 - Sample dope sheet from one of my animations.

When we create animation there are often multiple levels of art. Characters may be on separate levels. One character may be spread across multiple levels, like having a body on one level, a head on another level, a mouth yet on another, and legs on yet another level.

So for every frame - and there's 24 frames per seconds when you shoot on film - there might be 5, 10, 20 levels of art. One second of animation could consist of hundreds of drawings. There is a very specific way of numbering each drawing for each frame.

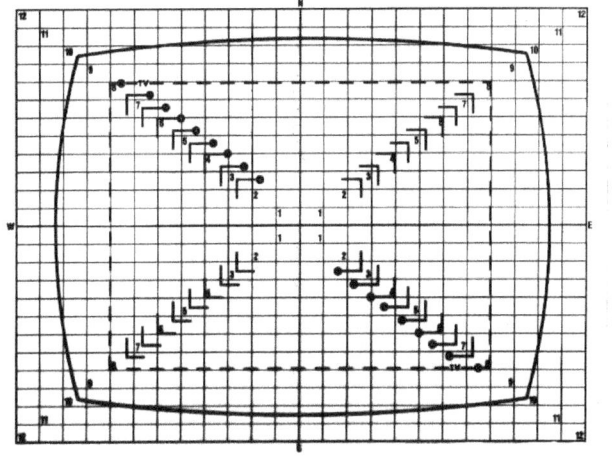

Figure 59 - Field Guide. The fits over your peg bar and helps the animator designate movements according to how many squares the camera moves in any direction.

To add another complication to creating a workable dope sheet, you also have to properly notate any art or camera movements.

The area of a film frame is broken into fields. Fields are concentric rectangles centered in the frame. If you have a drawing that needs to move, you mark how many fields north, south, east or west it needs to move.

I understood that process when I moved to LA. The problem is I understood only my self-taught process, not the

149

industry standard. Everyone else in the world worked differently than I did, I just didn't know it.

After I graduated from college I visited LA before I finalized my move. While there I went to an animation studio called Filmation to apply as an animator. Filmation was located only a block from an apartment where I planned to live. They produced shows like *He-Man and the Masters of the Universe*. It was a place where I really wanted to work.

I walked in without an appointment, introduced myself and spoke to one of the producers. I told her I was an animator and pitched myself. She smiled and said, "Let's give you a test - an animation test - see how you do."

That's common in the industry. Give someone a brief test to see if they really can animate. Sure. I was excited. No problem.

She gave me a scene for *He-Man and the Masters of the Universe*. I loved it, but I was also nervous.

The problem was I was just visiting town, so I didn't have an animation disc to work on. I sheepishly told her, "I'd love to do this. I don't have anything to draw on."

I couldn't believe her response. She actually lent me an animation disc. She had never met me before, but she handed me an expensive animation disc to use. I didn't even have to sign for it. She just handed it to me. Obviously, I had to return it, but she trusted me with it.

I took the disc, thanked her and I left to buy some animation paper and pencils.

I was staying with a friend at her apartment and I realized that I also needed a light source to put under the animation disc. A disc without a light under is almost useless because when you draw on animation paper, you need to be able to see through the multiple pages to line up each drawing as you sketch out the motions.

My friend didn't have a light table. She wasn't an artist. So I had to be creative. But, she did have a glass-top breakfast table. I placed one of her lamps under the table and propped up the animation disc on the table so it was at an angle I could draw on. I literally scabbed together a really cheap, fast animation stand. And it worked great.

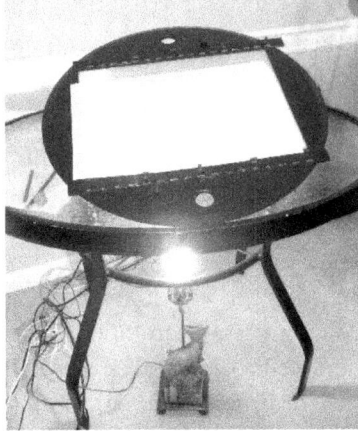

Figure 60 - The quick set-up for the animation disc the studio lent me. I put a light under a glass table to assist me in animating.

Production had given me a background and a few animation key frames, the main drawing poses to work from. The scene had He-Man running down a hallway and then he needed to slide into an elevator, stop and have the elevator door close behind him.

Easy enough. I finished the animation and had a great time doing it. I wrote out the dope sheet to plot the drawing positions and timing. I tracked the fields on the background to plot the perfect movement. I thought, "This is awesome. They're going to love it. I'm going to get hired immediately."

After a couple of days, I delivered the completed scene and returned their animation disc. I thanked the producer profusely for lending me the disc.

The producer took my scene and gave it to one of the camera guys to shoot my test. At that time, in the mid-80s, everything was shot on film. I didn't stay because they had to shoot and process the test film. It would take a couple of days before they could see my test.

I followed up a few days later. I arrived at the studio and sat down with the producer.

She said, "Well, the art looked okay, but you're not ready to animate. There were a lot of problems with the scene."

I asked, "What do you mean there were a lot of problems?"

"Well, nothing lined up. The character movement didn't match the background movement."

I discovered that instead of He-Man sliding to a stop perfectly inside the elevator, I had He-Man running through the back of the elevator.

I had overstepped my knowledge. I realized too late that working your way up and understanding how an industry functions can actually be a helpful thing.

So, there are times when attempting to start at the top may not be the best idea.

Chapter 32
I Assumed Control and Was Shot Down

If you've read this book from the beginning, you know that I ran my father's construction company when I was a teenager. At the same time I also started my own advertising company. All through college I published my own magazine and hired others to help on the mag as well as my advertising company. In other words, I was used to running crews and had done so most of my life.

When I moved to Hollywood after college, my mindset was still that I ran things.

My first job in Los Angeles was at a set building company called Serrurier and Associates. They were the top set building company in Hollywood. I figured that my route into live-action production would be through my ability to design and build sets, but I didn't know how Hollywood built sets. The first month-and-a-half I worked there, I stayed in the shop, learning. But I really want to be out on the sound stages.

I finally got my chance. One of our foremen asked if I'd go and help them break down a big set, which means to take down and dispose of the set that had been built, for a Mercedes Benz commercial.

I hopped in the company truck with a few other guys and we drive over the hill and down into Hollywood. The set to dismantle was on the Paramount lot, my first time working there. The Paramount lot where they shot *Star Trek* and *Cheers* among other great shows.

And then I remember driving into the studio through the front gate, through that historic big arch, and thinking how freaking cool it was.

We got out of the truck and I looked over my left shoulder to see the Hollywood sign in the hills looking down at me. It literally gave me a chill down my spine.

We walked into one of the sound stages and inside were large flats, false walls of the set, which we needed to take down. The flats were standing around this collection of six incredibly gorgeous Mercedes-Benz. The cars ranged from new to 50 years old. There were literally millions of dollars worth of cars sitting on that stage. I asked one of the guys on our crew, "When are they going to move the cars so we can get the sets out?"

He replied, "We can't get them to move the cars. Only one person has the keys and he's not available. We have the take the set down without touching any of the cars.

I love a challenge.

I stood there and looked around. The first thing I always do is take in the entire picture of whatever project I'm on.

I turned to our crew and said, "All right. Fred, why don't you come over here, and you and Bill grab that? Jim, you and I will grab this piece over here. George, I want you to make sure that that piece is held up from behind."

I gave directions to our crew on what each person needed to do and everyone started doing as I said, except for George, our foreman - the guy who was actually running the job.

George looked over to me with a grin on his face. He walked up to me and quietly said, "Mark, you're not running this crew."

And I just froze, and realized, oh shit, I overstepped my position.

I looked at George and said, "I am so sorry. I didn't mean anything by it. I am just so used to running crews."

He replied with his hand on my shoulder, "It's fine. I get that. You obviously are good at just taking control, but this is my crew."

"I got it. I got it." And I sheepishly walked away with some of the other guys as George started telling us what he needed us to do.

I was lucky that he didn't get mad at me. But I still wanted to run that crew.

Chapter 33
I Blew A Connection To SpongeBob

Years ago - probably late 90's - I had landed an offer for a TV series my wife and I had created from a company up in Canada called Alliance Atlantis. When I got that offer in writing, I used that offer to land an agent to represent me and negotiate the deal.

With a deal that important, I didn't want to negotiate it on my own. I also didn't want to work with a huge agency where I would be forgotten in a week. Gersh was one of the really good second-tier agencies and I thought would be a good fit for me. I called the main number and said, "I have a contract for a new series and I'd like someone to negotiate it for me."

The receptionist put me on hold. A minute later John Bauman picked up the line. John was one of their agents. He confirmed that I had a contract in writing and he signed me while we were on the phone.

Agents are not in the business to break new talent. They only get paid when a deal closes and gets funded. So, they tend to only work with seasoned pros who are more likely to land deals. They prefer to work with clients who are easier sells.

I wasn't giving John promises. I had done the hard work already. I had pitched a project and got an offer in writing. He could negotiate it and earn a commission immediately after signing me.

Agents are great to have for a couple of reasons. One, they negotiate your deal and they should get you more money than you would get without them. So even though I pay them a portion of what I make, I make more money overall because they can negotiate better deal.

But they also serve another great function. They can put their different clients together to create a bigger deal. If they can take client A and client B and put them together to create a package deal, the agent can make twice the commission for the same amount of work. If they package enough of a deal, they can also get a packaging fee from a studio. There's a lot of financial incentive for agents to package talent they represent.

So, John called me up one day and said, "Mark, you used to work at Nickelodeon, right?"

I said, "Yeah, I was one of the art directors there."

John asked me, "Do you remember Tim Hill?"

I said, "Sure, I know Tim. He was writer and producer on *Welcome Freshmen*. I designed *Welcome Freshmen* for him for four years."

Figure 61 - A set I designed for
Welcome Freshmen at Nickelodeon.

And he said, "What would you think if I paired you up with him on other projects?"

Without thinking of the benefits, I opened my stupid mouth.

If I could reach back in time, I would slap myself, "You know, I don't think so. Tim, I found he was pretty weak at Nickelodeon. It's not like that we didn't get along or fight or anything, but I was always having to get more information

156

from him and he would hide from me in his office because they were always late with scripts."

Now, it was relatively early on in my TV career, I didn't realize that scripts are always late in TV, because you're always trying to perfect them. I did hunt Tim through the halls of Nickelodeon so I could get the info I needed to design the episodes. I didn't think about what he was dealing with. He probably looked at me like a bully.

So my inexperienced ego said, "No. I don't think that would be a good idea."

Here's the problem - two problems actually. One, John never offered that kind of deal to me again. Two, Tim Hill went on to write and direct the *SpongeBob SquarePants* movie.

Now I'm not saying I would have gotten on the movie, but if I had reconnected with Tim and I hadn't let my ego get in the way, we could have worked together on bigger projects. He's written and directed a number of projects and is quite accomplished. Because I turned down an opportunity and let my ego and inexperience get in my way, I missed some huge opportunities. I'd say that's a major fuckup.

So just be careful on what you say about people, and how you react to situations and look at the bigger picture. I didn't realize it at the time, but my stupid comment hurt me.

Tim, if you're reading this, and I don't know why in the world you would, I'm sorry.

Section 7
Screw It – I'll Do It Myself

There are times when working with others is the smartest thing to do.

There are also times when doing it yourself leads you to new opportunities.

Other times you may find that the commonly accepted way of doing something is wrong and you have to venture out and create your own process or path.

And sometimes you get tired of paying other people to do something you can do yourself.

Following are stories which fit each of these times.

I probably do too much on my own. But I learn from it all and I can afford more in my life if the only person I have to pay is myself.

But in any case, doing something to prove you can do it, can lead to great things.

Chapter 34
How I Accidentally Sold My First Book

Simply asking questions and talking about your goals can lead to amazing things. While selling a book can be hard, my first book sale was quick, easy and unexpected.

I never thought that I would write text books. I knew I would create books of some sort because I love telling stories. I love comic books and comic strips. Comic strip artists were my original heroes. It was never the sport stars. Heroes in my life were always Charles Schulz, Hank Ketcham, Jim Davis, Johnny Hart and Berkeley Breathed among others. These are the guys who created my favorite comic strips; *Peanuts, Dennis the Menace, Garfield, B.C.* and *Bloom County* respectively.

While I have been a cartoonist, it was my experience in the film and TV industry that led me to write my first book. I had some things I wanted to say and wanted to share what I learned about art directing movies.

I started in Hollywood as an art director (after a brief stint building sets). I loved designing sets that told the story of a character. I loved the challenge of enhancing an existing location. It was fun to create the look of an entire movie, even on a low budget.

The benefit of working on low budget movies is you have fewer people handling more areas of production. As an art director, I was personally involved in every design, every location, every prop, every special effect and all the set decorating. I learned it all under fire.

I had looked for books about art direction and only found one book which in 1988 was already over thirty years old. A newer book was needed. Plus, the book I found only dealt with design, not about all the other aspects of working as an art director.

I had been art directing for a number of years when I decided to write about it. I wanted to share my knowledge of how to run an art department. The actual logistics of designing a movie, running a crew, dealing with practical effects, accounting, everything we deal with during a production. No other book had been written which covered this.

It was at that time I also starting to give lectures, so I figured a book was also something I could sell. So, I started writing the book.

The writing process went well, but I didn't have a plan on how to print it and distribute it. I wrote it in the early 90's, so digital printing was not available yet.

I figured I would publish the book myself. No particular reason, I just never considered pitching it to a publisher. One problem I had was I didn't know anything about distribution or printing books. I'd never done it before.

I did some research at bookstores and found that there were only a couple of publishers who published film and entertainment textbooks.

The books I liked the best were published by Drama Book Publishers. I figured if I was going to learn from anybody, I might as well learn from the best.

I found their phone number in the front of one of their books. I called and asked to speak with the owner Ralph Pine.

I was connected to Ralph and I started asking him questions. "Who do you use for printers? Is there a software that you guys use for laying out books? How do you approach book stores?"

For some reason he kept answering every question. He was being very nice and very open with giving me awesome information.

After we'd spoken for a bit, he asked, "Why are you asking all this?"

I said, "Well, I've got a book that I'm writing that I wanted to self-publish."

He asked me what my book was about.

I told him I was a movie art director and I was writing a book about the entire process and the entire art department in making movies.

He said, "Oh, really? In what way?"

So, I start telling him a little bit about my background, how I've been doing mostly movies, with some commercials, and some music videos. I shared how much of the book I had written and why I wanted to write it, to fill a hole in the industry.

The tables had turned and he was then asking me questions, "How are you laying out the book? What kind of chapters are you putting into it?", etc.

We'd been on the phone for almost an hour when he paused for a moment and said, "I like your book."

That was great, but I asked, "What do you mean?"

He said, "I'm interested. I think I'd like to publish your book."

"No shit?"

"Yeah. Why don't you send me a draft of what you've got?"

The call didn't turn out at all like I expected. I just wanted information on how to self-publish. Instead, my first phone call to a publisher ended with an offer to publish my book.

A day or two later I sent him my incomplete manuscript. I wanted to strike while the iron was hot and he was interested. I didn't know if he would be as interested if I waited.

That's when I first discovered that you don't need to have a completed manuscript to sell a non-fiction book.

Ralph called me a week later and said, "Your book looks great. Let's go ahead and do it." He sent me a contract.

I usually have a plan for everything I do. Landing my first book deal was not one of my plans. But, because I started at the top and spoke directly with the leading publisher in my field, I put myself, and my book, in the perfect position for something amazing to happen. And it did.

Figure 62 - The cover of my first book, Art Direction for Film & TV.

Chapter 35
Reinventing Resumes

There are times when you can start at the top with a new idea. Something that changes the norm. Sets a new standard. I did that with resumes.

When I first took a course in college on business and how to write a resume, nothing they taught about resumes made any sense to me. It wasn't logical at all.

Because of that, I sat down and rethought the entire purpose of a resume and what would actually work. So I changed what resumes are. In fact, I ended up writing a book with my wife and best friend called "Your Resume Sucks!"

It's the perfect title, because most of them do.

The way we look at resumes is that they should work for the person looking for the job, not for the employer who looks for reasons to say no. The only purpose of a resume is to get you in that door for the interview. That's it. Then you'll never need it again. It's up to you and your abilities to have a great interview and to land that job.

So, right out of college, I wrote my resume my way for all my freelance job searching. My resume was completely different than everything I had been taught, and it worked. It worked great.

My best friend, Jim Irvine, studied psychology. Jim had been out of school for a couple of years when I was talked to him about his job search, "So how's it going?"

Jim replied "You know, I'm working, but I can't get the job I'm looking for, you know, nothing in my career."

"Well, let me take a look at your resume," I offered.

He sent it to me. It was awful. It was bland and read just like every other college graduate resume. At a glance I saw employment gaps and out-of-date dates of relevant jobs. I didn't actually even know what he wanted to do from reading it. I had to ask him.

A quick note on all resume books but two, mine and one other. Most resume books NEVER MENTION JOB TITLES. That's right. The single most important part of a resume, and it's never mentioned. Not in books. Not in classes.

Do you know what is taught to be the most important thing on top of your resume? Your name. WRONG. No one is ever looking to hire a Jim, or a Jeanne or a Mark. They are looking for a Sales Associate, a Marketing Director, a Storyboard Artist. Put that on top of your resume. Otherwise, it probably won't even be read.

When I have to hire someone, I don't have time to read through a huge stack of resumes and try to determine what someone can or wants to do. I flip through a stack of resumes and pull only those with the job title I need to fill. If you don't have a job title on your resume, I won't read it.

That's just ONE example of the dozens of things that are taught wrong about writing resumes.

Back to Jim's story.

I questioned him, "Do you mind if I completely re-do it? My way? I want to totally re-do this, completely, from top to bottom because I think everything you're doing is wrong."

He shrugged and said, "But that's the way we were taught."

"I know, but let me do it my way."

I re-wrote Jim's resume and he had his dream job within two weeks. That was kind of proof that - besides my own successes - it really did work.

Over the years I refined how to write a resume that works for you and decided to write a book. The *Your Resume Sucks* book.

Figure 63 - The resume book I wrote with my wife Jeanne and my best friend Jim Irvine.

Jeanne and I brought Jim on - since the process worked so well for him - to be a co-author and to do the research proving that our ideas are better. Jim - at the time of this writing - is a hiring and training manager at Nissan USA. He has hired thousands of people. For Jeanne and I, not only have we hired hundreds and hundreds of people on all the different productions we've worked on, but we've also gotten hired hundreds, or in my case, thousands of times. So we're able to see what works in resumes from both sides.

After we had our children, Jeanne had stopped working on time-intensive productions for a while and wanted to get back into the workplace. I had some friends over at Disney in their advertising area - Disney Yellow Shoes Creative - and I suggested that she try to get a job over there.

Side point. A Disney HR (Human Resources) person attended a talk I gave at a college about how to write resumes. She came up to me after my talk with an angry look on her face. She told me point blank, "No one will ever get a job at Disney with your type of resume. It won't work. What you're telling people is the wrong thing, and it will never work."

I smiled, but obviously I disagreed. I've seen it work in every imaginable type of career. When Jeanne was home with the kids, she wrote resumes for people. We've helped doctors and attorneys, artists and sales reps and people getting hourly jobs or salary positions, you name it.

So Jeanne went in to Disney and used her resume, written our way, to apply for a job at Disney. She got a job there as a manager using the exact type of resume they said would not work. How's them resumes? *(a shout out to Matt Damon for co-opting and bastardizing his famous 'How's them apples?' line.)*

So, when I look at things like resumes or anything I disagree with, I am more concerned about how things should work and how to get things done efficiently. Not how it's always been done.

I didn't learn how write a resume from a book, or school or from other people. I learned by looking at a problem a different way. And now my book is used in colleges across the country.

Chapter 36
$3 Million in Publicity

Another way to start at the top, is to replace someone with yourself.

Years ago, I had hired a publicist to work with us, to help us with refining our message and getting stories out about all the different cool things that we were doing.

But having a publicist can be very expensive. They do a great job and it's very helpful, but for a small company it can be hard to afford. I couldn't afford to keep her on for every idea I had, but I wanted the publicity.

Now, for those of you not that familiar, publicity is free advertising. It's a story that will be printed or aired or onlined (is that a word?) at no cost to you. It could be on the radio, on TV newscasts, in newspapers, in magazines, online blogs, wherever.

Figure 64 - Cover story about my company in the Orlando Sentinel. Acts as an ad on the cover of a major newspaper. Huge value.

Publicity can be very, very helpful. Every business needs advertising to be successful. I don't know about you, but I'd rather promote my business for free than pay for it.

So rather than just give up on paying for her to get us publicity, I approached our publicist and I said, "I can't afford to keep you on. But I want publicity. I want to hire you to teach me how to do your job. I'm not going to compete with you, but I'm not going to hire you anymore. So I'd like to give you some more money now, to teach me how to do it for myself."

Probably not what she wanted to hear. Of course part of her argument back to me was, "Why would I teach you to do that?"

I replied, "Because I'm not going to be hiring you anymore anyway. At least this way, you'll earn a bit more."

She thought about it and agreed and taught me how to write my own publicity.

As a quick tip, publicity can't just be an ad. You can't just try to sell something. It needs to be a story that would be interesting to the demographics of whatever media you approach. For instance, if you won a big award, or donated something, or the subject of your book is relevant to some big news story. If their reader or listener are interested in your or your product/service, they'll reach out to you.

Figure 65 - Holding a 4-page magazine article about my career.
The cost of 4 full-page ads would be much more than I would ever pay for.

Over the years I've gotten well over $3 million in free publicity. I have appeared on *The Talking Dead*, Fox morning shows, NBC news shows, on covers of newspapers and magazines and in podcasts.

You can see some of the press I've gotten at http://storyboards-east.com/press/

Not everybody can write and develop their own publicity stories. There is a huge value to working with a professional, who can not only write press releases but has the contacts to get them distributed, but because I am also a seasoned writer I was able to take her information and be able to institute that for our own stories.

Promotion makes you look like an expert in your field, which can lead to great advancements in your career.

Section 8
Constructing the
Ultimate Attitude

There are times when constructing the ultimate attitude, or having the ultimate attitude, could work for you better than talent or ability.

I'm not saying you should ignore training or improving, but a really strong attitude translates to confidence, which inspires confidence from others. If you have a great attitude, employers will feel more comfortable with their decision to hire you.

Following are examples of how I have created an ultimate attitude, and how I use that attitude to help me in my career.

An attitude that will start you at the top.

Chapter 37
You've Been Doing It Wrong
For 20 Years

Doing something for a long time does not necessarily mean someone has been doing it the best way all that time.

I was placed in a position of authority when I was very young. I ran into a number of experienced workers, who didn't always know the best way to perform their job.

I was 14 when I started running my dad's home construction business. I ran the work crews. I was on the job sites every morning and made sure everyone knew their tasks and I also handled all the repairs on our homes.

It was funny because I was the only kid who would actually drive to junior high. I would often drive to our construction sites in the morning before school to get them started. There was no student parking when I drove to junior high, so I just parked with the teachers. After school I would go back to the job sites to close them down in the afternoon and drive home for dinner. This continued through high school.

I would drive our truck to the job site without a license (until I got a worker's permit at 15). As per Dad's advice, I just didn't do anything that would give a cop a reason to pull me over, so I never got stopped or got a ticket. But I could barely see over the steering wheel. I was probably about 5'-1" at the time.

*Figure 66 – My work truck in front of one
of our houses under construction.*

Young and short does not make for an easy job telling
large construction men what to do. They can be physically
imposing and they like to throw their weight around.

My dad was the owner of the company, so people paid
attention to me because they had to. That helped me build
confidence. But that only went so far when I was the only
one on the job sites. Construction dudes respond to size and
can smell weakness.

I knew what I was doing on the site. I grew up in
construction. Dad taught me well.

But knowledge will only go so far when directing a 6'-
5", 350 pound workman. They often didn't want to listen to
me. They would try to use their size to intimidate me. This
happens in life in all areas. Larger people want to intimidate
others.

To help get my wishes across, I built a deep, resonating
voice. I sounded bigger than I was. I still do.

I also had an attitude of knowledge and control. I would
stand toe-to-toe with these guys when telling them what to
do. I learned to be direct and not take any shit.

There was one time when one of our guys was doing

something, I can't remember the details, in an inefficient way. I knew a better and faster way. I approached him to show him the better way.

His response? "Listen punk, I've been doing this job for 20 years and..."

I cut him off. "Then you've been doing it wrong for 20 years. This is a better way to do it."

He glared down at me. I held fast and stared back up at him, not giving an inch. Small body, big attitude. If you back down once, they will always expect it.

He finally relented and tried my approach. It worked.

To cement having control in situations like that, I find that you need to give something back. Don't be a dick about it. I thanked him for trying it, which made him feel good about his decision, even if he didn't have a choice.

You win a couple of those battles, and you build respect.

Chapter 38
Act Like You Belong

To get access to the people at the top, you need to act like you belong wherever you are.

I've worked in the entertainment industry now for over 30 years. I've enjoyed working on feature films, TV series and commercials on both coasts.

Besides working in the industry, I'm also a really big fan. I geek out at the sets and the actors and the directors.

Back in the '80s, when I lived in Los Angeles, a bunch of my friends came out to visit. I wanted to show them some cool Hollywood behind the scenes.

On earlier movies I had designed, I would go to Universal Studios to visit their onsite prop house to find props. To get onto the lot I would give my name and the title of whatever movie I was on to the guards. I would tell them that I was there to go to the prop house. They would let me it.

It had always been pretty easy. No one ever checked the validity of the movie I said I was working on. I figured I could use any movie name.

I decided to take my friends on a private tour of the Universal Studios backlot. We all piled into my truck and off we drove to Universal. We got to the gate and I made up the name of a movie and said we were going to the prop house.

My friends tried to keep straight faces and had bet whether or not my plan would work.

The guard handed me a pass for my dash and the glories of Universal, it's sound stages and backlot were open to us. I drove us through the famous *Back To The Future* city square and around the sound stages. (this trick no longer works. They've enhanced their security, dammit)

Figure 67 - This was taken on one of my excursions around the backlot at Universal Studios with my friends.

I noticed Dan Aykroyd walking into one of the sound stages. I pulled over and grabbed a few clipboards from the back of my truck. I handed them to my friends. "Carry these and look like you know what you're doing. Follow me."

We walked up to door with our official-looking clipboards and walked right past the 'Closed Set' sign on the door. We walked directly into the sets of *Caddy Shack 2*. Movies have large crews and nobody knows everyone on a set. You just need to stay out of the way and look like you belong.

We spent an hour on set watching them shoot the movie and no one ever questioned who we were.

After I moved to Atlanta, I was working on *The Walking Dead*. One day we were shooting on location on the backlot of Tyler Perry Studios. I finished my work early, but I wasn't ready to drive home.

Instead, I drove to the sound stages and production offices on the lot where other productions were working. I was already on the lot and wanted to take advantage of that. I was new in town and wanted to meet other producers and production managers for potential work.

Figure 68 - The stages at Tyler Perry Studios.
I drove around to the other production offices
when I was there on The Walking Dead.

Some of the production offices were empty, but I found the offices of a scripted series that was in prep. I grabbed some of my promotional material and simply walked in. I followed the signs to production. No one stopped me, but a few people said "hi".

I walked right up to someone at a desk and asked to speak with the producer. He asked, "Sure. Can I tell her who you are?"

"Yep. I just moved my storyboard studio to town and wanted to introduce myself. I'm Mark Simon."

I find it's best to be direct. Don't beat around the bush. Know what you want and clearly ask for it.

He chuckled and said, "Wow. No one has ever just walked in before. Cool." He then stood up, led me to the producer's office and introduced me. I had the opportunity to share my samples with the producer and gave her my promotional materials and contact info.

Act like you belong and be direct in what you want. Get yourself where you need to be and tell people what you want. Clarity of message also exudes confidence.

Chapter 39
I Get My Kicks

A great attitude can set expectations from others around you that you're going to do well. That will only help you.

I used to compete in Tae Kwon Do as a national competitor. Every time I competed, I would compete in forms, a dance-like series of memorized punches, kicks and blocks that simulate a fight. I did forms mostly because I didn't like getting hit and kicked when sparring. Sparring hurts. I don't mind hitting other people, I just really don't like it when they hit me back.

Figure 69 - Competing in Tae Kwon Do Nationals.
I was the loudest and most intense in my performance.

Forms are a beautiful art form. It's like you're fighting an invisible person.

When most people compete in forms, they go through the steps: punch, pause, kick, pause, turn, block, pause. Very mechanical.

However, whenever I would compete in forms, I would compete against a vicious, invisible opponent. My face would change to a scowl, I'd get loud, I'd get really tense, and I would yell loudly on every attack. I would hit and attack with full force. I would react as if I was getting hit.

But my attitude started before my routine, my form, and end after it. My attack attitude would start the moment they called my name.

The way a forms competition works in martial arts is, everyone gets called at the same time when they compete against each other. You all march in together - single file - and surround the ring where you compete. We take a knee around three sides of the mat. On the fourth side are the five judges. There's the center judge and then two to either side. The center judge is the highest ranking judge, and they vote on a one to ten point basis on the quality of your form.

When they call your name you get to your feet, bow, walk around the opposite side of the mat or the ring from the judges, bow again, step in, bow again, walk forward, present yourself to the judges with a "kya" (a grunt), announce your name and the form you were going to perform. You ask their permission to begin, they nod their approval, you bow again, you back up to your starting position, and you begin your form.

Figure 70 - I am sitting on the left next to the ring, waiting my turn to compete.

Most people are rather quiet during the initial steps. Not me. You could see and hear my attitude the moment they called my name. I wanted to make sure every single person in that auditorium knew that I was there, and that I was there to compete and to win.

They would call my name, "Mark Simon." I'd hop up quickly to my feet.

I would pop up off my knees and I would yell out loudly with confidence, "Yes, sir." I would bow, and I'd run, not walk, to the far side of the mat, and when I would approach and present myself to the judges, I would grunt really loud. I would make my announcement, "It's a GREAT day for martial arts. My name is MARK SIMON and I'm here to perform Dalee Hyung Som Chong!" When the judges gave me the okay, I'd step back and I would give a huge yell when I was about ready to begin. They'd give me the nod, and I would start with bang.

I was in a battle. I would perform and make each move as strong and as hard and as loud as I possibly could. Every eye in the auditorium would turn and look to me, and I would finish in a fury. I'd usually be completely out of

181

breath from my performance.

After a couple of years of performing and competing with that intensity, I entered my last Nationals competition. As I entered, I walked up to a bunch of guys who I had competed against before. They asked me what division I was competing in that year. I said, "I'm in the executive division now that I've gotten older." A couple of the guys looked at each other and their shoulders and heads fell, and one of them said, "Oh damn, I guess we're competing for silver."

What that said to me was that my attitude on the competition floor convinced everyone that I was the one to beat. They felt I had already beaten them, and they were just fighting against each other for second because they weren't going to match my attitude or energy on the mat.

A couple of people did approach me and say, "Maybe you're being rude yelling and being that loud in front of the center judge."

I didn't worry about that. In the previous competition I had won, my center judge was the highest ranked female in the world, Master Sell. She was also the head of our entire Tae Kwan Do organization. My sensei asked her at the end of that competition, "What did you think about Mark and the way he presented himself? Do you think he's too loud or presumptive?"

Master Sell's response was, "It shows that he's confident. His performance and energy told me instantly he knew what he was doing."

When I competed with my attitude, the judges were impressed. I basically started with the highest score and points would be deducted if I had any mistakes. Everyone else started at zero and had to build up their score.

You want to win in life? Present a confident attitude and start at the top with a ten.

Chapter 40
Is It OK To Be Cocky?

When I first started working in Hollywood on movies, I moved quickly up to the position of art director on my first movie. Being cocky helped me become art director on my second movie.

I got hired on my first job as a construction coordinator on a movie called *Slave Girls from Beyond Infinity*, which was shot at Roger Corman's lumberyard studio (as it was nicknamed) in Venice, California. It's the same studio where so many luminaries in our industry got their start, from the actor Jack Nicholson to director Jim Cameron.

Two weeks into working on *Slave Girls*, I became the art director of the movie. As always happens in production, the job only lasts so long and you need to go looking for another job before you know it.

Figure 71 - I am standing, in the black shirt, with part of my crew on the set I built for Slave Girls From Beyond Infinity at Roger Corman's studio.

After *Slave Girls* ended, production manager, Devorah Hardberger, had landed a job as production manager on another low-budget feature on a movie, called *Deathrow Gameshow*.

Devorah really liked working with me on *Slave Girls*. She saw I was a hard worker and I was able to make a lot out of a very small budget. Since *Deathrow* also had a small budget, Devorah said to co-producer Glenn Campbell and director Mark Pirro (as she told me later), "Let's bring Mark in. He could do the same thing for us as he did on *Slave Girls*."

Devorah brought me in to meet with Mark and Glenn. I met them at Mark's condo. I felt very comfortable in the meeting since I had just worked with Devorah. I was joking around with them and I let them know that, no matter what came up, I'd be able to deal with it. My whole life has been proof of that, so I had no problem being direct about it.

I was pretty cocky in the meeting. I knew what I could do and I had no problem telling them that I knew what I could do. I felt that everything went well in the meeting. As I left they thanked me for my time and said they would let me know.

A few days later, I spoke with Devorah and asked her what Mark and Glenn thought of me and if I was going to get the gig.

She said, "Well, it was funny. When you left, the other two looked at me and said, 'Wow, he's pretty cocky, isn't he?' I said, 'Yeah, he is. But do you think he'd let anything keep him from accomplishing what we ask him to do?' They thought for a moment, looked at me, and said, "No, you're right. Let's bring him on." She laughed.

And I got the job. I got the job because my cockiness, without being a dick, gave them confidence that I would move hell and high water to create and pull together anything and everything possible for their movie.

I didn't try to play it calm, cool and collected because that could come off as not interested. I let my excitement of designing a movie come through in the interview. I showed to them how much I cared about what I was doing, how much I really wanted to art director for them. I had no problem telling them what I was good at and how I had figured out ways to create the impossible on *Slave Girls*.

*Figure 72 - A giant set on Slave Girls From Beyond Infinity
that we could not afford to build, so it was created with a
foreground miniature of everything above the lower level.*

Sure, part of it came off as cocky, but cocky is often looked at in the wrong way by some people. It's even harder for self-confidence women.

If you can back up your own praises, it shouldn't be called cocky, it should be called confident. And that's okay. Don't let someone saying you're cocky make you quiet down. Let it work for you. Own it. Accept it.

*Figure 73 - One of our sets from Deathrow Gameshow,
which was the 2nd movie I art directed.*

Epilogue

Part of the trick to Start at the Top, is to be prepared. Know what you want and know as much about it as possible.

Eh eh, no excuses. Sure, you have to study. You have to practice. You have to be prepared.

But studying doesn't have to be hard.

Ever hear a kid talk about their favorite video game? No? Just talk to one. They know every detail, every fucking minute detail of every game they play. They know every special move of every character. They know every stat. Every character Damage-Per-Second (DPS). Every tactic and every setting.

How did they learn so much? They learned by playing the game. But they also watch YouTube and Twitch videos (LinkedIn Learning for you). They read online articles and Instagram posts by pro players. (sounds a lot like studying, doesn't it?)

It wasn't hard for them to study and remember these details. They have an interest in it. We all need to fill our lives with careers and hobbies and people with what and whom we have just as much interest.

With knowledge, inspiration, attitude and opportunity, you too will be able to Start at the Top.

Thanks for reading. If you enjoyed this book, please leave a review on Amazon.com.

Mark Simon's Other Books

You can find more details on Mark's books and lectures and all sorts of interesting things about him at www.MarkSimonBooks.com

Storyboards: Motion In Art, 3rd Edition

The bible of the industry, used at schools and studios around the world. Used by beginners and seasoned pros alike. Covers every aspect of storyboarding from the art of the craft, to the business of boarding, pricing, how to get started, tricks of the trade, interviews, exercises and over 1,000 samples. No other book on storyboarding comes close to this one.

Your Resume Sucks!

Everything you thought you knew about resumes is WRONG! Your resume needs to work for YOU, not the employer. Resume writing secrets revealed through an entertaining story. Before and after examples of resumes are included.

Facial Expressions

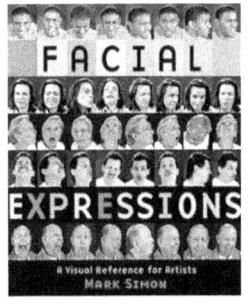

Facial Expressions is a series of photographic reference books for artists of all styles. The first in the series, featuring adults ages 20-83, includes over 3,200 photos of 50 models. Other galleries included feature kissing, phonemes, hats and headgear, skull and more.

Facial Expressions – Babies to Teens

The follow-up print book to the best-selling Facial Expressions series, Babies to Teens, features photos of 63 models ranging from 3 weeks old to 19 years old. Other galleries include skulls, hats, phonemes, age progression and more.

Mind Your Art & Animation Business

by Mark Simon

Fun articles about serious business. Earn more money in your creative business. Covers all creative endeavors. Based on Mark's hugely popular articles, Mind Your Business, as seen in Animation Magazine and Animation World Network (AWN).

DIY TV Pitch Kit

Do you have a TV concept to sell...or want to someday? Imagine how much faster you could sell your idea for a TV show if you had a step-by-step, easy as 1-2-3, course on everything you need to do to get your show ready to pitch and info on how to get those coveted pitch meetings.

Producing Independent 2D Character Animation

Producing
2D Independent
Character Animation

MARK SIMON

Step-by-step production of an animated short from concept through pre-production, production, post and then what to do with your finished piece. Takes an in-depth look at the artistry and production process of cel animation in a friendly, how-to manner that makes the sometimes tedious process of animation enjoyable and easy to understand.

Mark Simon's Live Talks

http://www.marksimonbooks.com/lectures/
Mark has spoken at events around the world on topics ranging from business and promotion to storyboarding and animation to pitching and selling.
Here is a brief description of a few of his talks.

How I Got More Than $3 Million In Free Publicity

Mark Simon, entertainment industry expert, gets thousands of dollars in free publicity every month. Discover his secrets and increase the exposure for your property.

Start At The Top

Inspiring stories from Simon's book of the same title, and a few extras stories that he held back.

Pitch Like A Pro

The best idea won't sell without a great pitch. Learn what is needed in a great pitch and what to avoid.

Storyboarding

Discover the secrets to storyboarding from the Godfather of Storyboarding, Mark Simon.

Land More Freelance Jobs

Job Search MYTHS Exposed!
E-mailing resumes WILL NOT land you freelance gigs.

Mark Simon's
LinkedIn Learning Courses

https://lnkd.in/marksimon

Course –Storyboard Pro Essential Training

Course – 3D Storyboarding with Storyboard Pro

Course – Wacom Tablet: Customizing ExpressKeys

Course – Voice-Over for Video and Animation

Course – Using Character Animator in Production

About the Author – Mark Simon

Pitch Expert & Godfather of Storyboards

Everything in Mark's life revolves around telling stories. As a pitch expert and co-owner of Sell Your TV Concept Now, Inc., he works with content creators to craft pitches which will enthrall potential buyers. Mark has been hired by Disney, Nickelodeon, The Golf Channel, HSN and other networks to help pitch in-house productions. He has also developed and pitched IP created with Jeanne Simon and inked 40+ production and distribution deals.

As a storyboard artist and owner of Storyboards & Animatics, Inc, he teams up with film and TV directors to bring their visions and scripts to life. He is best known for his work as the storyboard artist on *The Walking Dead, Dynasty, Miracle Workers, Cipher,* and dozens of feature films for Universal, Fox, Warner Bros. and most recently Jon Favreau.

Mark is a 30-year veteran producer and director for live-action and animation and has piled up an impressive 5,000 production credits.

As much as Mark pushes his storytelling, he also pushes himself to excel in digital storyboarding. He won a 2012 Prime Time Engineering Emmy for his work with the Toon Boom software team behind Storyboard Pro. He was also inducted into the DAVE School (Digital Animation & Visual Effects School) Hall of Fame.

Mark is not only a storyboard artist, he is an in-demand instructor and has produced multiple training courses for LinkedIn Learning, formerly known as Lynda.com.

Books are another chapter in Mark's story. He has penned eleven industry texts on storyboarding, animation, and several photographic artist reference books.

He has traveled the world telling stories and sharing his expertise as a lecturer at major pitch conferences, entertainment industry trade schools, and universities.

As the father of identical twin young men, he has filled their hearts and minds with stories about how to live a life doing what you love.

The answer to the question you have right now is NO... he doesn't get much sleep.

His storyboard and animation clients include: The Walking Dead, Disney, Universal, Viacom, Sony, HBO, Nickelodeon, FOX, Starz, Steven Spielberg, USA Networks, ABC Television and many others. He was the animation producer of Universal's *How High 2*, Fox's *Tooth Fairy 2* starring Larry the Cable Guy and Universal's 2014 release of *Little Rascals*.

You can reach Mark at MarkSimonBooks@yahoo.com